APOCKETFUL OFBEACH HOUSES

APOCKETFUL OFBEACH HOUSES

Edited by Stephen Crafti

images
Publishing

Published in Australia in 2009 by
The Images Publishing Group Pty Ltd
ABN 89 059 734 431
6 Bastow Place, Mulgrave
Victoria 3170 Australia
Tel: +61 3 9561 5544 Fax: +61 3 9561 4860
books@imagespublishing.com
www.imagespublishing.com

National Library of Australia Cataloguing-in-Publication entry:

Title:	A pocketful of beach houses / editor, Stephen Crafti.
ISBN:	978 18647 0348 1 (hbk.)
Subjects:	Vacation homes.
	Architecture, Domestic.
Other Authors/Contributors:	Crafti, Stephen, 1959-
Dewey Number:	728.72

Coordinating editor: Andrew Hall

Original text by Stephen Crafti, Robyn Beaver and Dianne Strong

Designed by The Graphic Image Studio Pty Ltd, Mulgrave, Australia
www.tgis.com.au

Digital production and print by Everbest Printing Co Ltd. in Hong Kong/China
140gsm Gold East matt, with 40oz caseboard

IMAGES has included on its website a page for special notices in relation
to this and our other publications. Please visit www.imagespublishing.com.

Contents

Peeling Back the Roof

ALEX POPOV & ASSOCIATES

Photography by Kraig Carlstrom

This three-storey house, clad in cedar, is relatively modest compared to many new homes on the cliff tops. 'Our clients didn't want a palatial home with all the trappings of the city. They wanted a beach house, somewhere to escape to at the end of each week,' says architect Alex Popov.

While the cliff top site offers spectacular views over the beach and headlands, it is unfortunately orientated away from the sun. To address the issue of light, Popov designed a skillion-shaped roof made of zinc, and to ensure direct light entered the house, he 'peeled' back the roof and inserted highlight windows. 'The roof is like a can that has been ripped open on one side,' says Popov, who was able to draw in the light as well as views to the cliff face.

As the house is nestled into the cliff face, the entrance is at the top level. This level includes the lounge, kitchen and dining areas, together with the main bedroom and ensuite bathroom. This open plan area is protected by generous roof overhangs and by electronically operated metal louvred screens that control the harsher light. The middle level comprises three smaller bedrooms for the children and a bathroom and the ground level features a games room and shower. The ground level also leads directly to the swimming pool.

Even though the house is substantial in size, it doesn't dominate the cliff face. The base level, finished in cement render, also reduces the scale of the house. 'We didn't want the house to overshadow other houses or the beauty of the vegetation'. As Popov says, 'It's clearly not a 1950s cottage by the sea. But it's a long way from the house the owners leave behind in the city each week, both in distance and aesthetically'.

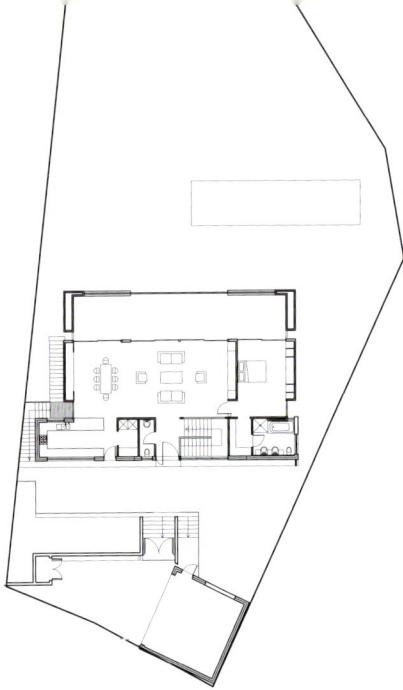

Cliff Top Rapture

ANDERSON ARCHITECTURE

Photography by Nick Bowers

Perched on the cliff top at Ben Buckler's Point, North Bondi, the six-unit 1930s apartment building has seen many changes over the years, including part of the property collapsing in the recent past. The owner of this particular apartment wanted a more liveable and sustainable environment, better connected to its dramatic natural surrounds.

The layers of the sandstone cliff under the building are a metaphor for the layers of complexity in this residence. While on the surface the apartment feels sleek, modern and contemporary, a tremendous amount of work was carried out to bring it up to this state. The project started by exploring the existing plan, which included a small, poorly oriented, south-facing living space and an oversized kitchen. To optimise the space a more desirable east orientation was achieved by enlarging and combining the living and dining spaces. The reshaped layout resulted in the majority of walls within the apartment being rebuilt while still using the support of the original planning as preserved in the apartment below. The layout had to use all of the original services penetrations in the slab – the toilet, for instance, is in the same location but rotated 180 degrees.

The apartment originally had four main windows, but because the sills were a metre above the floor, the water views disappeared when the occupants were seated. The solution was to cut the sills down to floor level and to install high-performance, low-E glazing and stainless-steel balconies. These new windows reconnect the bedroom and living space to the ocean, virtually bringing the ocean and the environment inside the apartment. A further benefit of the new openings is increased light by day, while low-wattage T5 coffer lighting is used to provide lighting at night. The changes to the window openings complement the building's fenestration and are now the key feature of the apartment and a major contributor to the transformation. To further accentuate and blur the connection to the ocean, the lightweight acoustic floor, finished in limestone, continues outdoors and the balustrades are fitted with frameless glass.

Site Specific

ASHTON RAGGATT MCDOUGALL

Photography by John Gollings

This house on Victoria's Westernport Bay is surrounded by 80-year-old banksias, with views of the ocean directly ahead. Designed by Ashton Raggatt McDougall (ARM), the original plans for a new house centred on the panoramic vista, with typically large picture windows. However, to preserve the banksias, as well as respect the sensitive sand dune setting, ARM subsequently decided to take a different approach. 'We wanted to create a more understated quality,' says architect Ian McDougall, a director of the practice.

The owners, a couple with three children, wanted a place that would be a refuge. They also wanted a place that was fairly communal. 'They're a musical family and it was important for them to come together and perform, whether piano or violin,' says McDougall.

As the site has a fall of approximately 7 metres to the beach, the house was positioned close to the road to maximise the views and minimise disruption of the vegetation. An uncovered deck at the front of the house is used for parking, with the front door approached indirectly via an extended deck. 'It's not a classical approach,' says McDougall, referring to the off-centre position of the front door.

Past the threshold, a more expansive view of the site is offered. Stained black cedar cladding acts as an important frame to the house, as do extensive decks that wrap around the upper level. Internal plywood walls and ceilings, which appear to have been cranked into position, set up views of the bay. 'It's quite an organic design. There's a plasticity to it, where the walls and ceilings have been moulded,' says McDougall, pointing out the different ceiling heights in the open-plan kitchen and living areas.

Part of ARM's brief included creating a reasonable distance between the parents' and children's bedrooms. As a result, the parents' bedroom, including a walk-in dressing area and ensuite, is located on the top level, while the three children's bedrooms, bathroom and separate play area are located below. But rather than both levels being symmetrical, the lower level has its own setbacks, in line with the trees on the property. 'We were determined to retain all the established banksias on the site. The irony was one of the largest banksias blew over in a storm after the foundations were laid,' says McDougall.

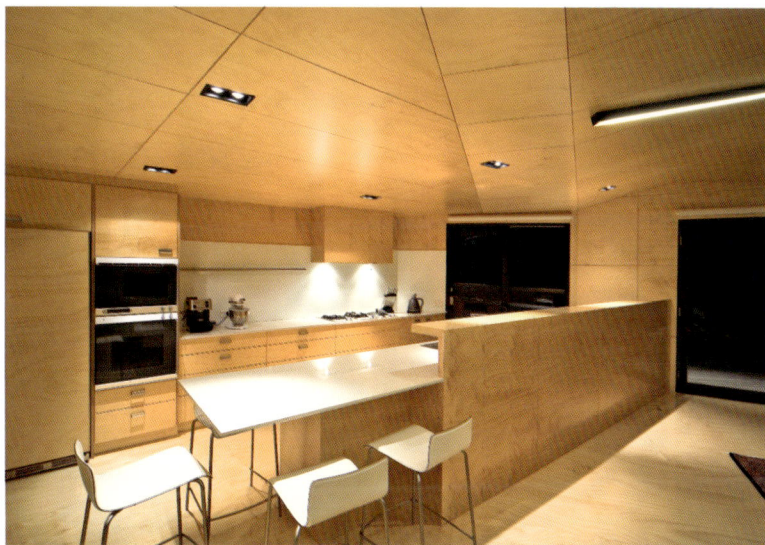

The Letter K

ASHTON RAGGATT MCDOUGALL

Photography by Peter Bennetts

This house, on Victoria's Bellarine Peninsula, was designed by Ashton Raggatt McDougall (ARM) for clients who wanted something challenging. 'The owners weren't afraid of new concepts. They embrace new ideas,' says architect Howard Raggatt, one of three directors of ARM, who worked closely with project architect Sophie Cleland.

The owners, a couple with two grown children, had few requirements in their brief to the architects. There was a request for separation between adults and children as well as a separate study and generous bookshelves for the owners' significant collection of books. Given carte blanche to experiment, ARM came up with the letter K as a possible form for the new beach house. 'There are two parts to a design. One is to respond to a brief and the owners' needs, together with looking at the site. The other is creating a strategy that will tease out some of the more complex ideas,' says Raggatt.

The ground level, comprising the home's 'shadowy' base, is made of concrete block work and partially clad in dark grey timber. The first floor appears slightly lighter, constructed of timber and painted a lighter shade of grey. As striking as the building's jagged edges are flashes of red beneath the soffit and ceiling to the carport and undercroft. While vibrant red is restrained on the exterior due to local planning guidelines, it's expressed within the home, both at ground level and on the upper levels. The ground floor includes a carport, also used as a covered outdoor area, two bedrooms, a bathroom, cellar, storeroom and a home cinema.

A staircase leads to the first floor, with its extraordinary bright red K-shaped bookshelf, which forms a wall as well as part of the balustrade. Integral to the 17-metre-long open-plan living, dining and kitchen area, MDF gloss shelving creates an entirely new concept for arranging books. 'Our clients enjoyed seeing these esoteric designs. Many people have difficulty looking at quite abstract ideas,' says Raggatt, who included suspended bookshelves in the study, accessed via a spiral staircase adjacent to the kitchen.

ARM's K house is more than the representation of an interesting letter in the alphabet; it a dynamic beach house, with easy access to the beach and shaped to shelter the owners from the wind.

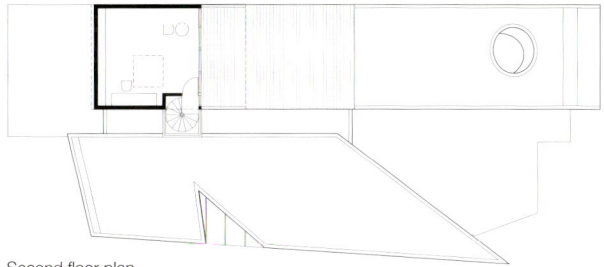

Second floor plan

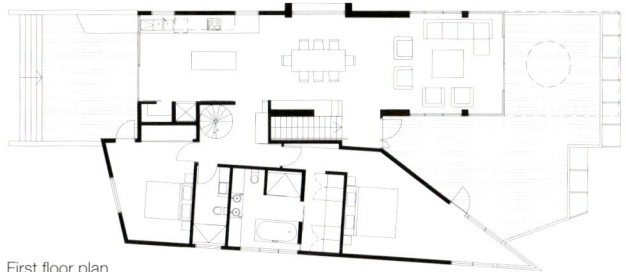

First floor plan

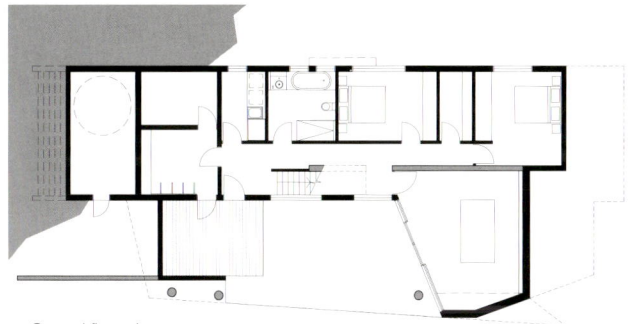

Ground floor plan

0   3m

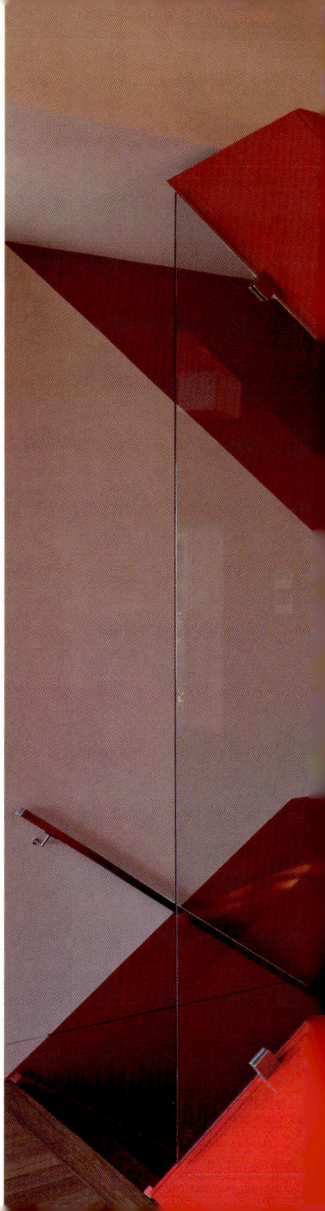

Controlling the Views

B.E. ARCHITECTURE

Photography by Trevor Mein

This house at Flinders, on Victoria's Mornington Peninsula, is buried deep into its 4-hectare site. Invisible from the street, the cedar-clad house only appears at the end of a long winding driveway. 'We wanted to control the views over Bass Strait rather than present just one vista,' says designer Broderick Ely, director of B.E. Architecture.

Designed for a couple with two adult children, the brief was to create a large house with a focus on entertaining. 'It's almost two interconnected houses,' says Ely, referring to the separate guest accommodation comprising three bedrooms and a living area with its own kitchenette.

However, it is the main pavilion, with an open-plan kitchen and living area that draws the immediate accolades. Featuring 5-metre-high ceilings of painted timber and floor-to-ceiling glass windows and doors, there is a sense of connection to the rolling hills and Bass Strait in the distance. 'We've tried to personalise each view, whether it's from the living areas or from the main bedroom,' says Ely.

The main bedroom, conceived as a separate two-storey wing, is linked to the living areas via an enclosed breezeway. On the first floor are the main bedroom, ensuite and dressing area. Below is a cabana/gymnasium that leads directly to the swimming pool. However, rather than elevate the pool, it is positioned below a 35-metre-long stone wall. 'You really only see the pool when you lean over the rock wall. We didn't want it to detract from the larger vista,' says Ely, who also used the stone wall to create a plinth for the covered terraces above.

Four outdoor terraces create a series of informal rooms around the house. Featuring cypress posts and a polycarbonate roof lined with timber, these outdoor terraces merge with indoor spaces. While the house is contemporary, inspiration was drawn from rustic buildings built in America in the 1920s. 'I visited a library in Colorado. In one of the books I picked up were old photos of buildings constructed in rough stonework,' says Ely, who wanted to introduce similar textures to this Australian house.

A Private Retreat

BAILEY ARCHITECTS

Photography by Kallan MacLeod

This region of Northland, New Zealand, is predominantly farmland. However, the area is also known for its beaches, many of which, like Lang Cove, are relatively protected from the elements. Only an hour-and-a-half drive from Auckland, on the east coast of the North Island, Lang Cove is a popular destination for weekenders.

This house, located at the southern end of the beach, is only separated from the sand by a 50-metre-wide grassed reserve. Like most popular beach resorts, there are houses either side. 'Our clients wanted privacy from neighbours. They wanted to feel as though they were on their own, at least when they're inside the house,' says architect Jason Bailey, director of Bailey Architects. Privacy was achieved by using carefully positioned fin walls to maintain lateral screening without blocking the views.

The original timber home on the site was mostly demolished. Walls from the original garage, together with a small amount of structure surrounding the entrance were incorporated in the new building. The new two-storey house is a combination of materials: painted pine weatherboard combined with in situ concrete for walls, plus glass and aluminium. Aluminium louvred screens form an important component of the design. 'It's quite a calm environment, but the site is fairly exposed. We wanted to ensure the house could be adjusted in response to the prevailing winds or sunlight,' says Bailey, drawing across one of the external aluminium louvred screens on the terrace.

As the house is at the end of a relatively steep drive, one steps down from the garage into the main living area on the ground floor. The ground floor also includes a kitchen to one side of the living areas, a bedroom and separate office as well as a laundry and powder room. The main bedroom, on the first floor, has a large sitting area as well as a large terrace. The mezzanine-style bedroom also benefits from views over the lounge and across to the beach. 'The house was designed for a couple with adult children. They often come here on their own,' says Bailey, who didn't want the house to feel over-scaled. 'The upstairs is almost self-contained,' he adds.

Upper level floor plan

Lower level floor plan

Equis House

BARCLAY & CROUSSE ARCHITECTURE

Photography by Jean Pierre Crousse

'We believe that to inhabit the desert, it is essential to 'domesticate' the landscape without denying or betraying it. We decided to begin the design process by imagining an abstract and plain volume whose limits are defined by building regulations. Then, during the design process, we excavated this volume, removing matter as archeologists remove sand to discover pre-Columbian ruins in this region.'

This 'subtractive logic', very different from 'constructive logic', was applied to all scales of this Barclay & Crousse Architecture project. The result was exterior spaces merging with interior spaces in a continuous fluid space within a precinct, where landscape and sky are each framed in different ways. The entrance patio leads to the intimate space of the house. This space extends toward the ocean with a large terrace, which is conceived as an artificial beach that relates to the ocean by a long and narrow pool.

The living/dining space roof is conceived as a weightless beach umbrella, anchored to the precinct, and the barriers between the living/dining space and the terrace are erased by frameless glass sliding panels. An open staircase follows the natural topography and leads to the bedroom level beneath the terrace. The children's bedrooms are accessible by a patio/pergola covered by the terrace deck, and the parents' bedroom is reached at the end of the staircase, passing under the suspended pool.

The use of ochre and sand colours, found also in pre-Columbian and colonial houses, prevents the building from visually aging as it gathers layers of desert dust and reinforces the sense of unity of the excavated volume. The long distance between Sandra Barclay and Jean Pierre Crousse's office in Paris and the Peruvian site led them to rationalise the construction system, and detail work that appeared not to be essential was eliminated. The remaining details were simplified so that they could be easily built by local craftspeople.

A Black Lighthouse

BELLEMO & CAT

Photography by Mark Munro

A 1950s fibro shack once stood on this site at Point Lonsdale, on Victoria's Bellarine Peninsula. While the house was too small for the owners, a couple with two children, there were elements they fondly recalled. 'The typical beach shack of that period featured under-cover car parking. It was something they were keen to have in the new house,' says architect Michael Bellemo, a director of Bellemo & Cat.

The new house, measuring approximately 230 square metres, was conceived as two structures connected by a large deck. 'Our clients wanted a separate study that could also double as a retreat, either for parents or when the children are older,' says Bellemo, whose inspiration for this structure came from a black lighthouse at Queenscliff, a historic town a few kilometres away. The 7-metre-tall study/retreat could also be compared to Australian bush hero Ned Kelly's helmet, with a picture window framing gnarled tea-trees.

The primary form of the house is rectilinear. The main bedroom and ensuite are located at the front of the house, cantilevered over the carport. The main living areas, including the kitchen and dining areas, are at the centre, creating a buffer between the children's bedrooms and informal living area to the rear. A floor-to-ceiling lime-green door separates the two living areas.

The home's north and west elevations are clad in sugar gum timber, stained black. In contrast, the south and east elevations have been finished with fibro cement sheeting and painted in a leaf-green colour. 'Black intensifies the landscape,' says Bellemo, who was also keen to create a link to the past by using fibro cement.

Although the site was relatively undisturbed during construction, an established acacia was removed from the front garden as it was blocking the entrance. In memory of the tree, Bellemo & Cat infused the design with a variety of green hues. An awning made of polycarbonate was designed with computer-generated images of leaves. Memories of the tree are also captured in the glazed bricks used in the fireplace, separating the living and dining areas. 'We're not trying to replace the tree, but it's important to make connections to the past,' says Bellemo.

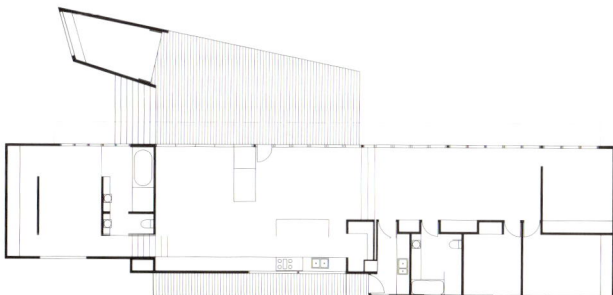

An Angler's Idyll

BEVIN + SLESSOR ARCHITECTS

Photography by Nicholas Bevin

This new bach replaces an earlier, self-built, 'low-slung' family bach. The design was conceived as a single and simple gabled form reminiscent of the hull of an upturned fishing boat. This form allowed the floor space and volume to be maximised within the site's planning restrictions.

Living spaces were kept open-plan on the ground floor and were positioned to the east and north to maximise access to outdoors and the sweeping coastal landscape views. Large bi-folding doors allow the extension of the living area onto the deck and allow uninterrupted views to the beach. Timber louvres each side allow for adjustable ventilation in the east wall.

The main bedroom upstairs takes in spectacular views of the coast while a secondary living space doubles as additional sleeping space when required.

The open space behind the bach catches the last sun of the day and provides for barbeques and 'after fishing' activities, protected from the regular summer evening on-shore breezes.

The selection of the exterior palette of materials was based on durability and relative low maintenance in the aggressive coastal environment. The robust palette is limited to stained battened plywood and cedar, powdercoated aluminium, glass, hardwood and corrugated Colorsteel.

Exterior corrugated screens have been designed to slide over the lower level windows, wrapping the bach up when not in use.

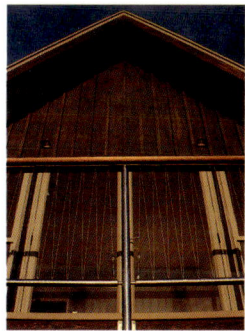

Balinese Influence

BLIGH VOLLER NIELD ARCHITECTURE

Photography by David Sandison & Neil 'Moonwalker' Amstrong

Located on the Sunshine Coast, Queensland, this house has a strong Balinese influence. Positioned at the end of a cul-de-sac on an established canal estate, the house features its own private beach. The house was designed for a couple, one of whom spent considerable time travelling through Southeast Asia. 'The brief included a sense of his travels, but he didn't want a pastiche reproduction piece,' says architect Shane Thompson.

While the house appears completely new, it was built on the foundations of a 1970s Spanish mission-style house. Some original walls were incorporated, but the original house has been extended considerably. The two-storey house now includes three wings interspersed with six bodies of water.

The first body of water is experienced in the front courtyard, where a bridge links the gate to the entrance. At the front of the house (facing the street) is a two-storey wing with a guest bedroom and garage. Above the garage and bedroom are four additional bedrooms, together with bathrooms. 'The owners' children are grown up, but they regularly stay, along with their children. And there are also overseas guests,' says Thompson.

Past this wing is a large two-storey reception area, offering views over a pond to the swimming pool and the river beyond. This central courtyard, with pond, contains a Balinese sculpture. 'The spaces are essentially organised around this courtyard,' says Thompson, gesturing towards the two additional wings. One of these wings comprises a series of sitting areas, with the main bedroom and ensuite above. The third wing is given over to the kitchen and living areas. The outdoor living areas, with generous canopied outdoor rooms, are further important elements of the design.

There are elements in this home that are derivative of a Balinese house, for example the ceilings throughout the house feature woven raffia mats, bought in Bali in a street market. Yet, while there are traditional Asian touches, there's also a contemporary feel to this home, with large timber and glass doors disappearing into cavity walls. 'Essentially, it's one large verandah,' says Thompson. 'The spaces are informal. Here it's about stripping away inhibitions and relaxing by the pool or the river,' he adds.

At One with Nature

BOORA ARCHITECTS

Photography by Laurie Black

This house stands at a threshold between forest and ocean, shade and sun, intimate glade and distant vista. These defining dualities were observed at the beginning of the design process from a clearing at the western edge of the narrow sloping site.

As a response to these conditions, the project strategically deploys service elements as opaque forms that direct diagonal views and define both communal and intimate spaces. Working with existing trees and topography, these forms create areas of arrival, privacy and shelter. The occurrence of these consistently detailed forms on the interior and exterior of the house unites inside and outside through similar shapes, textures and details.

Primary spaces are arranged along the narrow bar to receive southern light filtered through spruce groves and to capture ocean breezes for maximum cross-ventilation.

The first two levels of the house contain a studio and bedrooms. Concealed sliding wall panels and pocketed opaque glass doors contained within the opaque forms allow the spaces to offer maximum transparency or provide privacy when required.

The highest level contains living, dining and kitchen activities in a naturally lit space open to expansive views. Two decks extend this space further into the landscape – one toward the ocean, the other over the forest courtyard.

Natural materials are used in the garden walls, site work and architectural expression. A consistent and honest approach to detailing links inside and outside spaces while celebrating local skill and craft. All stone was found on site or obtained at a local quarry. Sensitive siting minimised soil disturbance; only two trees were removed.

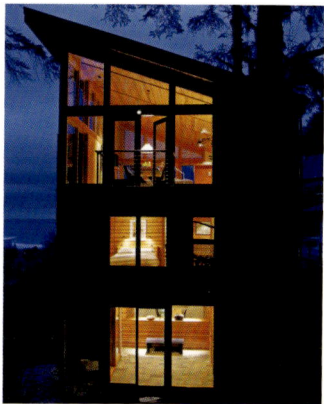

Designed for Two or Four

CENTRUM ARCHITECTS

Photography by Axiom Photography + Design

This beach house at Lorne, Victoria, was designed for a couple with adult children. 'Our brief was to design a house that would work for the whole family or just for two people,' says architect Ken Charles, who worked closely with fellow Centrum Architects directors Geoff Lavender and Alan Cubbon.

Overlooking Loutitt Bay, the site is as much about the shoreline as the hilly bush setting, dominated by established eucalypts. As the slope of the site is approximately 30 degrees, the materials used are fairly lightweight: timber and steel frames clad in Ecoply and solid timber straps. Painted a purple-red hue, the Ecoply evokes the colour of a sunset at Lorne.

Because of the steep slope, almost two-thirds of the land couldn't be built on. However, to maximise the building envelope, the house is spread over three levels. The top level, also the street level, includes a 'platform' for the parking of two cars, a study and entry vestibule. One of the most distinctive features upon arrival is the sculptural staircase made of timber, glass, painted board and steel rods.

On the central level of the house are an open-plan kitchen, living and dining area, all benefiting from panoramic views of the trees and water. There's even an impressive view of the water from the ensuite to the main bedroom. 'Providing water views from every vantage point was an important part of the brief,' says Charles.

Timber features extensively in the interior of the home. Recycled timber was used for the flooring in the dining area, extending to the outdoor terrace. There is also extensive timber joinery, such as a credenza built into the living area. 'It's a fairly robust house. If it's not built-in, then it's extremely solid,' says Charles, referring to the chunky timber table in the dining area.

On the lowest level, designed with separate access, are two additional bedrooms, a bathroom, a billiard room and gymnasium. There is also a second living area. 'The two floor plates are almost identical. The two areas can be used in their entirety or partially closed down if the owners come down on their own,' says Charles.

A Celebration of Timber

COX RAYNER ARCHITECTS

Photography by Christopher Frederick Jones

Elysium is a unique concept in Australian architecture. Conceived as a totally architect-designed estate, it brings together some of the country's leading and emerging architects. A short drive from Noosa, the only brief to architects by the developer was to ensure every house was different.

This house was one of the first to be completed on the estate. 'We wanted to celebrate the use of timber. It seemed appropriate being on the edge of conservation parklands,' says architect Rebekah Vallance, who worked closely with her husband, architect Casey Vallance, and architect Michael Rayner, director of the practice.

The house is almost entirely made of Australian hardwoods such as spotted gum. Timber battened screens and minimal windows in the front façade prevent harsher light entering the home, as well as creating privacy (at the end of a cul-de-sac). Past the front door, the house opens up to a north-facing courtyard and pool. 'The entrance is quite protective. We wanted a slow introduction to the house,' says Rebekah Vallance, pointing to the spotted gum timber on walls extending to ceilings. The timber screen framing the staircase provides an abstract reference to the strong verticality of the adjacent eucalypt forest.

The main living areas, with the formal lounge and dining area separated by the kitchen, are on the ground floor. The kitchen protrudes out to the terrace, also clad in timber. The extensive use of timber ties the house to its bushland setting with careful detailing emphasising the house's crafted quality.

Upstairs are three bedrooms and bathrooms, including a large main bedroom and ensuite. A media room leads to a Juliet-style balcony that pierces the central void over the staircase. 'It's a relatively large house for the site (approximately 500 square metres). To avoid an underutilised 'backyard', the intent was to create a seamless transition from interior to exterior, to ensure the outdoor living area was integral.

The northern terrace of this house acts as an indoor/outdoor room. The double-height space is protected from sunlight in two ways: via a translucent roof and by a tier of timber battens acting as a canopy. While there is a beach nearby, this house draws its strongest reference from the adjacent nature setting, creating an elegant beach retreat.

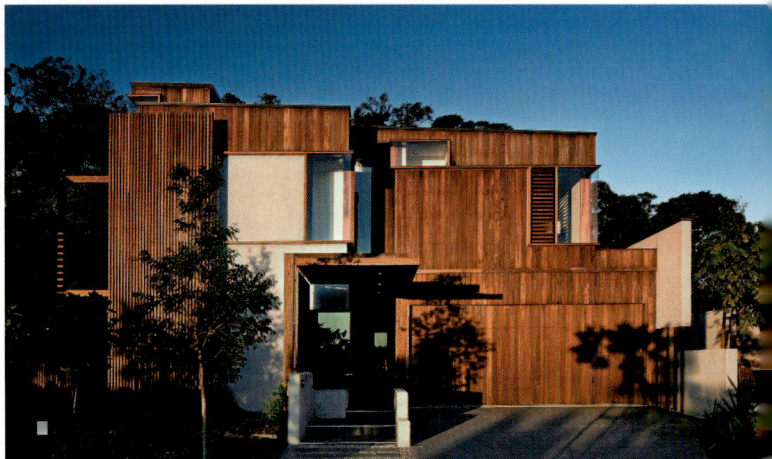

Panoramic Allure

CPRW FISHER limited

Photography by Simon Devitt

This weekender, overlooking Hahei Beach in New Zealand, offers panoramic views of the Coromandel and adjacent islands. Relatively modest in scale, approximately 200 square metres, the design is deliberately understated to emphasise the home's scenic location.

Designed by CPRW FISHER limited, the brief to the architects was to design a low-maintenance house for a couple and their children, who live most of the time in Singapore. 'They wanted something that was no maintenance, rather than low maintenance, a place they could simply open and close, like a suitcase,' says architect Michael Fisher, a director of the practice.

The timber-framed house features steel beams and is clad in Zincalume, as is the roof. The rectilinear-shaped house is spread over two levels. At ground level is the garage, together with the two children's bedrooms. On the upper level is the main bedroom, which is separated from the main living areas by an ensuite bathroom and second bathroom for guests. 'It's a fairly simple design. We wanted to go back to the idea of the original beach house, the one large room that everyone enjoys being in together,' says Fisher.

And like the original beach house, the design includes an open deck leading from the main living areas, as well as a covered deck for more inclement weather. Fisher included in the design sliding Zincalume doors to frame the windows as the winds can be strong. These can be pulled back during finer weather or drawn across to enclose the interior spaces as well as one of the decks. A cantilevered platform creates the impression of being anchored into the land at the rear of the site.

The materials used for the interior are low maintenance. The floors in the living room are plywood and lime-washed and the walls are made of plaster board lining and painted white. Even the flooring in the bathrooms, Pirelli-studded rubber, was conceived for low maintenance. As Fisher says, 'The exterior is hardy. It won't need painting. The zincalume will dull over time, merging with the surrounding vegetation'.

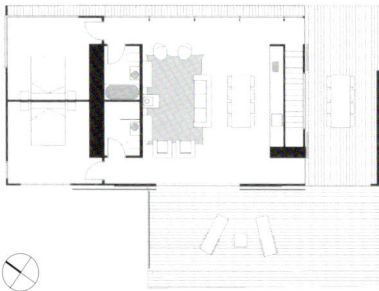

Maximum Exposure

CRAIG STEERE ARCHITECTS

Photography by Jenny Norton

The client brief for this beach house at the base of the Yallingup Beach hill was to create maximum space and accommodation for at least two families on the restricted site and to take full advantage of the spectacular coastal outlook.

The design and shape of the dwelling was a process of natural evolution, directly reflecting the strict constraints placed by the local municipality. From these formal restrictions the main staggered body and angular roof line followed the angled street boundary. The upper and lower viewing platforms were then twisted and orientated towards the main surf break to the southwest. This created a natural large cantilever in the balcony and roof planes to offer protection from the western sun and winter weather. Recessed outdoor living spaces were then sculptured into the building to offer protection from the prevailing sea breezes.

To enhance protection from the late afternoon sun and sea breeze, automatic external shade fabric roller blinds, controlled by sun and wind sensors, were fitted to the upper deck, discreetly retracting into concealed recessed troughs within the eaves' lining. An automatic reticulated window washing system was added to enable 'salt free' clear viewing, and to enhance the durability and life of the aluminium frames.

Simple, durable and practical materials, which offer a subtle but effective aesthetic value, were selected for the interior. They include polished concrete floors, walls finished in the same acrylic render used on external walls, chocolate-coloured Wenge-stained cabinetwork, resin-based terrazzo and limestone tiles. Similarly, durable and maintenance-free materials were selected for the exterior: heavy duty, extra coated Colorbond roofing, flexible coloured textured acrylic brick walls, in situ concrete paving. The materials create a minimal external palette that connects the structure to the coastal vegetation.

A Deliberate Orchestration

DALE JONES-EVANS ARCHITECTS

Photography by Ashley Jones-Evans & Stephen Blakeney

A generous triangular site overlooking the ocean was the perfect stimulus for a die-hard surfer to build his dream home. 'My client was looking specifically for the 'Bombie' (a surf term for the premier wave spot),' says architect Dale Jones-Evans who designed this extraordinary new house.

Accessed via a cul-de-sac, the site unfolds over a 25 per cent gradient and has a 360-degree view of the Indian Ocean. While Jones-Evans could have designed a house with views that provided instant gratification, he preferred to set up a journey where the experiences gradually unfolded. There were a number of significant elements in the landscape: 'There's the strong ridgeline of the landscape. It's almost like a floral sea. There's literally the sea and the crashing surf and also an intriguing church that was built in the 1950s, which forms an outcrop in the landscape'.

A small aperture in the home's front elevation (facing the cul-de-sac) is accessed via a banded horizontal path. Tucked in behind rendered walls, which act as a barrier to the prevailing winds, the entrance to the home is cave-like. 'It's like entering a citadel. You can't see around the building. It's a bunker that follows the contours of the land'. The 'bunker' contains the bedrooms and bathrooms, while the lighter component, the floating copper dome, includes the kitchen, living and outdoor areas. 'There are two opposite sensations of "bunkering into" and "floating over" the landscape. The building is designed to age and crust, the cement render will soften and leech salt and the copper will oxidise green,' says Jones-Evans.

Through a narrow slot in the kitchen wall there is a glimpse of what lies ahead. Standing in the kitchen, the picture unfolds, with the ridgeline and sky to one side, views of the church to the other. To ensure that the finishes do not distract from the design, Jones-Evans used concrete for the kitchen floors and for the terraces either side. Even the kitchen bench was designed in concrete. 'It's like one giant brushstroke,' he says.

The copper roof, which made the house a beacon in the area, was literally pulled down from 2.8 metres at the centre of the living area, to 2.1 metres at the edge. With the lowered ceilings, there's a cave-like experience when either entering the home or moving out onto its expansive patio. At the tip of the building, on the cantilevered patio, the entire landscape wraps around the house.

Designed from Afar

DANIEL MARSHALL ARCHITECT

Photography by Daniel Marshall

The architect of this house in New Zealand didn't meet the owners until the house was being constructed. At the time, the owners were living in the United Kingdom, planning a return to New Zealand to live permanently, and as such the design evolved by phone and the internet. The final stages relied on a DVD (an animated film) together with a physical model of the house, shipped over to the UK.

The initial brief for the house at Omaha, an hour's drive north of Auckland, was Cape Cod style. 'It wasn't a style our office is known for. We prefer creating contemporary homes,' says architect Daniel Marshall. As a way of finding a compatible path, Marshall suggested the owners look at a book on the contemporary architecture of the Hamptons, New York, for inspiration.

The site, perched above the beach, was also influential in the design. Because it is relatively exposed to the southeast winds, the architects felt a protected courtyard space was required. As a result, the cedar-clad and glass house features a courtyard garden, protected from the wind by a single-storey living pavilion. 'We wanted the owners to be able to look though the living areas to the sea, rather than feeling closed off,' says Marshall.

On the ground floor are the kitchen, dining and living areas, together with a second raised sitting area. The two living areas are separated by American oak joinery, one side functioning as storage, while the other side, the sitting area includes an open fireplace. At the front of the house, facing the street, are three bedrooms and a bathroom.

On the first floor are the main bedroom and ensuite, together with a dressing area. There is also a separate bunkroom. Marshall included a balcony, accessed via the main bedroom, to allow the sea views to be enjoyed at all times. 'It's a reasonably transparent house. The coastal dunes are integral to the design,' says Marshall, who included glass sliding doors in most rooms.

While the house isn't Cape Cod style, there are finely sculptured nooks within the essentially rectilinear form. The cedar plywood ceiling in the sitting area is faceted. And three smaller canopies protruding over the deck have a fine sense of craftsmanship. 'It is contemporary, but it's not just a minimal glass box,' says Marshall.

Time Out

DANIELA SIMON ARCHITECT @ SODAA

Photography by Robert Frith

Architect Daniela Simon wasn't looking to build a beach house for herself. 'But then a friend bought a block of land here. Even as I was driving down, I had no intention of buying,' says Simon, who couldn't see the point of travelling 530 kilometres south of Perth on a regular basis. However, when she visited the coastal heathland, it wasn't long until she signed a contract.

Situated on 4 hectares of land and adjacent to her friend's property, this house at Bremer Bay is next to the Fitzgerald River National Park. 'It's a ten-minute walk to the beach and only a short drive to the nearest township, Bremer Bay,' says Simon, who designed the house for her partner and three adult children. 'The children come down with us as well as independently,' she adds.

While Simon's initial thoughts were that she wouldn't use a beach house, she now regularly uses it. 'It's like paradise. It gives me a complete break from the city,' she says.

The house is relatively modest in scale. Approximately 140 square metres, it is conceived as an alternative to camping. 'I refer to it as "luxurious camping". It's a place to protect you from the wind and cold,' says Simon. Made of rammed earth and Corten steel, the split-level house was designed to accommodate as few as two and up to ten people. There are two enclosed bedrooms. And there are also beds on the mezzanine above the living room and in the living room itself. 'I wanted the design to be flexible. There's something quite special about curling up and going to sleep in the corner of a living room,' says Simon, pointing out a nook in the living room that extends beyond the walls.

Rammed earth appears on the exterior of the house and is expressed in the interior walls, including the kitchen. Rather than the usual red colour associated with rammed earth, these walls are grey. 'I combined the rammed earth with cement. I wanted the exterior walls in particular to disappear into the landscape,' says Simon.

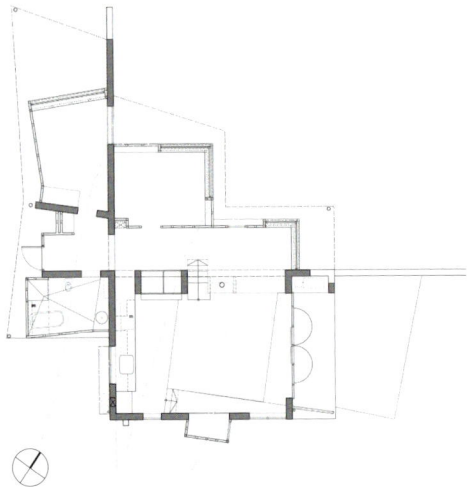

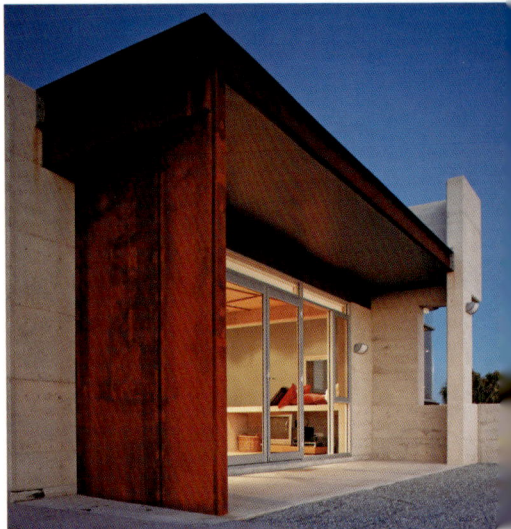

A Small Footprint with a Large Impact

DONOVAN HILL ARCHITECTS

Photography by Jon Linkins

Known by the locals as the 'T' house, this simple yet extraordinary home is a landmark in its small beachside settlement. Essentially an 8-by-8-by-8-metre cube, the architect's intention was to keep as much of the natural bushland intact as possible. Surrounded by national park, the landscape is relatively unstructured and undisturbed. 'Centralising the activity and accommodation into a single "box" ensures that the site boundaries can remain indistinct as the local vegetation converges on the building,' says Timothy Hill, one of the architects.

The design centres on a double-height outdoor room. Extensive enclosure and northern orientation ensures that the room can be used throughout the year, rather than only during the warmer months. Instead of solid masonry walls dividing the outdoor room from the bedrooms and living areas, the architects used translucent partitions. The natural light and shadows created by the partitions are quite dramatic, particularly during the summer months.

The timber house is designed over three levels, with entry from the dune into the house's mid-level. The undercroft level is for vehicles, energy services and storage. Entry gates to the living level open directly into the double-height outdoor room. The living level also includes the kitchen and bathroom. The upper level provides the main sleeping accommodation.

In this house, the architects designed compact built-in bed cubicles that enable the spaces to be used during the daytime. 'We wanted to give the rooms a "person-sized" appeal and for the owners to have the pleasure of sleeping near the landscape (individual hopper windows were designed at each sleeping platform)'.

Even in the outdoor room, there are protected nooks for those wanting some solitude. And surrounded by the native bushland, all the elements can be experienced first-hand. As Hill says, 'There are no surfaced roads or drainage services. The areas' character is largely a product of its "undevelopment"'.

On a Rugged Canvas

GEORGE EL KHOURI ARCHITECTS

Photography by Gregory Haremza, Max Dupain & Associates, George El Khouri

This house is located in an area rich in natural beauty. Rolling waves meet a rock cliff face against a backdrop of step-forested slopes of an escarpment that is at times covered in mist and fog. The sky forms an arc that binds these layers together.

The magnificent setting and scale led to a house that reflects its layered landscape. The layering concept influenced the conceptual decisions and then the planning and choice of materials and colours of the residence. The rendered proportions, stone feature walls, tiled blade entry plane, horizontal timber boarding and the strong linear flat roof tiles of the external façade mirror the unique layers of the landscape setting.

The planning theme of the house is carried through to the interior. The changing moods of light, reflection, shade and wind movement are captured in each room of the house, making each individual in the way it captures these characteristics. The simplicity in detailing and choice of materials provide a strong connection to the natural environment.

The interior room arrangement has been streamlined and altered to reflect the conceptual planning theme. Glass doors fold away to completely unite adjoining spaces; blinds are concealed above the windows; glass curtain walls open the living area to the surrounding environment to pull the views into the living space; unwanted glimpses are screened with floating blade walls and white obscure glass. Perception of spaces in the home change as one wanders through the house and glimpses different slices of the views outdoors. The entire house is clutter-free to maximize views.

The residence has been designed as two separate living quarters, with the upper level as the main residence. The ground floor can be separated for guest use but can also be used as an overflow of the main living area.

Consultant interior designer: RLD (www.rldesign.com.au).

Truly on the Beach

GODWARD GUTHRIE ARCHITECTURE LTD

Photography by Patrick Reynolds

This striking contemporary home is adjacent to a popular beach and harbour. With water views from most rooms, a sense of tranquillity pervades the house. 'Our client's brief was for a modern, casual home, to be constructed in low maintenance materials,' says architect Julian Guthrie, a director of Godward Guthrie Architecture. 'The clients also requested the primary living areas be located on the upper level to take best advantage of the outlook,' he adds.

Located on a long, narrow site, the house is elevated one metre above the ground. 'The house is located on a flood plain,' says Guthrie, who interwove the interior and exterior spaces at both levels to offer varying sun orientations, shelter from the winds and privacy from the beach road.

Entry to the house is through louvred gates. A glass bridge above the entry lobby leads up the stairs to the main living areas on the first floor. The main living area seamlessly connects to a teak floored balcony, with the ceiling extending out as a cantilevered fibreglass brise-soliel.

On the northern side of the house is a 'floating' wall, clad both internally and externally in pre-weathered zinc. 'The wall provides a screen to adjacent houses. It also creates a gun-slot window to the sea,' says Guthrie, who included several louvred screens at strategic points for privacy.

The ground level accommodation includes a living area, together with three bedrooms and a bathroom. 'We wanted to create a second living area that would connect to the pool and courtyard,' says Guthrie.

Focusing on the view, the house has been deliberately pared back. Interior finishes, for example, are monochromatic, with subtle changes in finish from solid plaster to fibrous plaster to lacquer, emphasising the shifting light and continuity of spaces. The garden is also pared back. It's a fairly harsh environment. So the architects used New Zealand native coastal plants such as New Zealand iceplant and cabbage trees as features in the landscape.

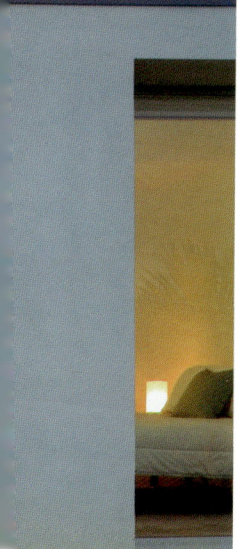

City Chic meets Coastal Calm

GREG NATALE DESIGN

Photography by Anson Smart

Palm Beach is the northernmost of Sydney's beach suburbs, located about 30 kilometres from Manly and less than an hour's drive from the CBD. Situated at the end of a landmark peninsula, it is home to many of Sydney's 'rich and famous' and boasts breathtaking views of the Pittwater, the Pacific Ocean, golden sandy beaches and pristine bushland. Luxurious homes and historic cottages happily coexist in this part-suburb, part-beach resort.

The clients' brief to the architects was for a relaxing, yet chic, home away from home for the entire family. They wanted to encapsulate the feeling of beachside living in all aspects of the interior.

The 200-square-metre house was an original 1950s beachside property set up high on a hill with panoramic ocean views. A mix of organic shapes and materials such as cane and timber was chosen as a bold contrast with the stark geometrics in the original carpet designs. Modern minimalist furniture and mid-century iconic furniture juxtapose the Asian-inspired florals and toiles; outside, a beachy, casual feel is accentuated with paddlepop lounge chairs and Milan stripe and paisley prints. The colour palette is restrained with the use of natural timbers, soft blues and yellows.

Out to Sea

GREGORY BURGESS ARCHITECTS

Photography by Trevor Mein

Designed by Gregory Burgess Architects, this house was the result of a limited competition. A number of architects were short-listed and asked to submit a scheme. The 10-acre cliff site, overlooking the bay, would have created an adrenalin rush for most of the competing architects.

Before submitting plans for this idyllic site, Burgess, who won the competition, workshopped a number of ideas with the owners. They wanted an extended beach house, which would accommodate three generations of the one family, either at the same time or independently. Unlike many houses, which include only the one main bedroom, this house was designed with four main bedrooms and accompanying ensuite bathrooms (two on the ground level and two on the first floor). 'They also wanted separate areas for the children to play, but without isolating these areas,' says architect Gregory Burgess.

Therefore, the three main living areas – the breakfast 'plate', the living area and deck, and the dining room – wrap around the kitchen area. The 'fire pit' in the living area, further delineates the open-plan living areas.

Burgess chose to site the house on the cliff face to provide the most dramatic outlook possible. 'The house is at the edge where the land starts to gradually fall away (there's a 30.5-metre drop to the bay below). We wanted the house to engage with the eastern edge, as if it was emerging from a wave,' says Burgess. The radially sawn yellow stringy-bark house, detailed with galvanised-steel balconies and handrails, features a flat-sheet galvanised-steel lookout. Reminiscent of a ship, the house has a strong prow-like quality.

In contrast to the more lightweight stringy-bark, which was designed to weather, the house features a limestone wall, arising from the landscape, arcing to the entrance. 'The low roofed wall connects and anchors the house's cluster of pavilions and directs you across a courtyard towards the main entrance and circular vestibule,' says Burgess. Instead of the entrance being clearly visible from the front of the house, Burgess 'buries' it. 'The limestone wall guides you into the house surrounding the vestibule from where you peel off to the various zones and levels.'

Like a ship, with a number of decks to explore, the generous landings and internal courtyards follow the contours of the land. And while there is an intriguing series of paths to follow, one of the most worn is the one that leads to the pool and spa area. The loose shade structure, covering the spa and partially covering the pool, appears like a palm frond that has just been brought home from the beach. Made of yellow stringy-bark, it creates dappled shade across the deck. While the sea is 30.5 metres below, the house has an aerodynamic presence. There is a sense of it cutting through the water at great speed.

The Sound of the Surf

HAYBALL

Photography by Peter Clarke

For this weekender, both client and architect preferred to 'hold back'. 'This house was designed as a retreat for our client. She has a hectic work schedule and wanted a place that was nestled into the bush,' says architect Rob Stent, one of the directors of Hayball.

Created for a fashion designer, the idea of projecting the house out over the winding beach was never entertained. 'We really saw the house as an escape; somewhere the client's teenage daughter could have friends to stay, as well as occasional guests,' says Stent. So when this vacant site, protected by a dune, came onto the market, there was no intention of creating a soaring glass box to demand the attention of passing motorists. 'We wanted to create several experiences in the house. It isn't just about entering into one space and having one view: the surf,' says Stent.

The house, which is made of plywood, messmate, aluminium and glass, is spread over two levels. The front of the house, comprising the upper level, contains the main kitchen and living area. Leading off this space is the main bedroom and ensuite, together with a small and protected deck. On the lower level is a casual living area with kitchenette, bunks, a separate bedroom and facilities for guests (a bedroom and ensuite). The second level was deliberately designed as a self-contained apartment. 'The house can be shut down in a sense if only one person is in it,' says Stent.

The notion of approaching the views from several perspectives is expressed in the main living area and bedroom. A balcony deck extends the width of the living area and offers the most brilliant views of the headlands and water in the foreground. However, when seated in the lounge, there are views through slotted windows of the rough bark of the coastal scrub.

While Hayball is recognised for large commercial projects, they continue to pursue specialised residential projects. As Stent says, 'We don't design many private homes. But we're always keen to include these in our schedule. They're like making models. It's an opportunity to explore detailing and new materials. These discoveries can then be worked into our larger projects'.

Enveloped in Colour

HAYNE WADLEY ARCHITECTS

Photography by John Gollings

Cape Liptrap in southeast Gippsland, Victoria, offers a sense of isolation. 'We had a small weatherboard house in the area for years. We loved the area, so it was simply a matter of finding the right place to build,' says one of the owners, who was captivated by views over Bass Strait and rolling tea-treed hills.

Hayne Wadley Architects were likewise impressed with the unique surrounds. 'It's not a typical beach aspect, with surf and breaking waves,' says architect Andrew Hayne, who designed the house with his partner Katherine Wadley.

The brief to the architects was fairly simple. 'The clients wanted a fairly modest house, approximately 250 square metres including the separate guest quarters, with one large combined kitchen and living area,' says Hayne, who manipulated the design to fit between two stands of tea-trees. The architect couple were also mindful of creating a form that would provide some resistance to the prevailing winds.

As a result, the house turns its back on the point of entry with the concrete block façade featuring only highlight windows. The main feature upon arrival is a vibrant red steel and aluminium helix wrapping around the house. 'We saw the helix as a way of binding and protecting the house from the elements,' says Hayne.

In contrast to the southern elevation, the entire northern aspect features floor-to-ceiling windows. Combined with a large deck and broad timber staircase, the northern elevation loosely takes the form of a grandstand. A considerably more curvaceous line appears in the black Colorbond roof that encloses the main bedroom and the west end of the house.

While the palette of materials and finishes is relatively simple, the architects were keen to activate the interior rather than create a passive backdrop to the 'theatre' in front. As a consequence, a curvaceous plywood wall in the main bedroom wraps around and is expressed in the living room wall. 'There is that sense of being enveloped. It's a unique location and we wanted to make the interior reflect that,' says Hayne.

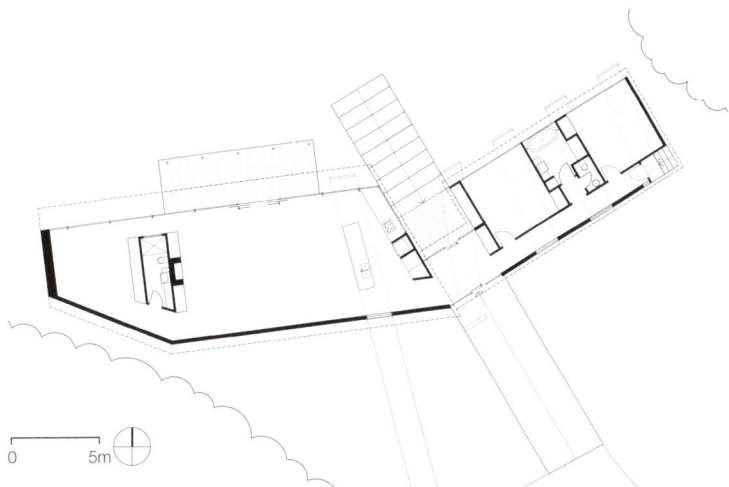

0 5m

Alfresco Living

HULENA ARCHITECTS

Photography by Kallan MacLeod

The owners of this beach house live on a farm in Hawkes Bay, on the east coast of New Zealand's North Island. 'Our clients wanted a place near the beach, where family could come together on weekends and holidays,' says architect Brent Hulena.

Southern Hawkes Bay is a comfortable 45-minute drive from the owner's home, but the coastal environment couldn't be more different. The hilly terrain is as dramatic as the surf beach. 'It's quite a desolate area. There are only a handful of houses,' says Hulena.

Although the children have left home, the brief was for a house with five bedrooms. 'There are also grandchildren on the scene,' says Hulena, who was asked to create one large living area where all the family could congregate.

As a consequence, the concrete (block), steel and glass house is designed in an L-shape. One wing, facing the water, comprises a 15-metre open-plan kitchen, dining and living area. Beyond the kitchen door are two bedrooms and a library. The shorter side of the L features another two bedrooms, one of which is used as a bunkroom that doubles as a second living area for grandchildren.

As the region can experience extreme winds, the architects designed two outdoor areas, one leading from the living areas to the beach on the east, the other to the west. The western courtyard is not only protected from the wind, but also benefits from views through the generous glazing on either side of the kitchen and living areas through to the beach beyond.

To strengthen the link between the indoors and outdoors, all the rooms open onto outdoor areas. When it comes to alfresco dining, bi-folding windows were incorporated in the kitchen, enabling easy entertaining to the eastern terrace. A fireplace in the western courtyard allows for comfortable evening dining. 'The house is used year-round, so it was important to create comfortable outdoor spaces,' says Hulena.

While the outdoors and indoors are blurred in this home, the living spaces are pivotal to the design. 'There's nothing better than just lying on the lounges and gazing out to the beach,' says Hulena, who included aluminium louvres above the glass doors in the living areas, as well as over the outdoor terrace, to control sunlight.

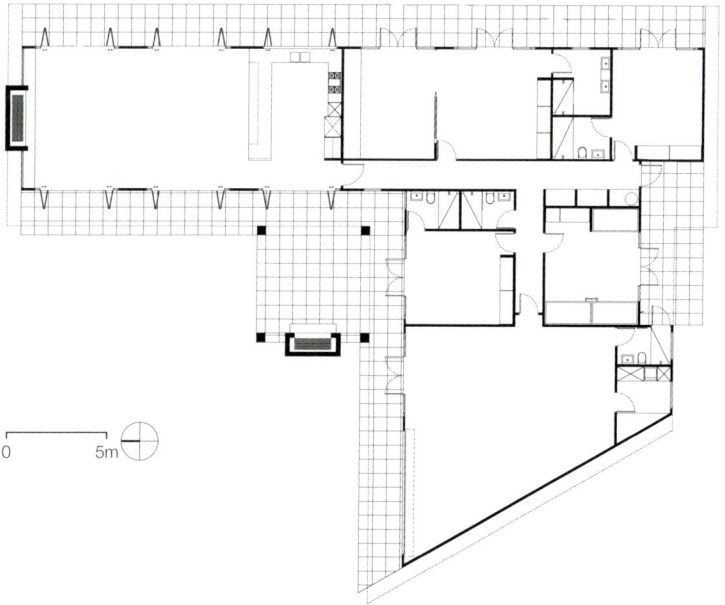

0 5m

A Journey

JOLSON

Photography by Scott Newett

Designed by the office of Jolson, this house is located above a golf course. While the course attracts golfers from around the world, so does the area's rugged coastline.

The 270-degree views over the golf course and surf are sensational, but so is the strength of the prevailing winds. With the inclement climate, it is understandable that the clients were keen on a concrete house. 'They wanted a solid home and had always wanted to live in a house totally made of concrete,' says architect Stephen Jolson, who designed the house with Adam Muggelton and Bianca Winter. Designed for a couple and their extended family, the 400-square-metre house (excluding garages and terraces) is divided into two wings, separated by a concrete catwalk or drawbridge.

On one side of the house are the main bedroom, kitchen and living area. The other wing accommodates the other bedrooms, including guestrooms, and the study. 'Our clients didn't want to feel as if they were occupying a large rambling house if they decided to come down and stay on their own,' says Jolson.

There are three distinct views of this precast concrete house. From the road, the house appears as a monolith, which has erupted from the ground. The raw exposed concrete follows the curves of the road. But through the front door, the house starts to reveal itself as the first part of a journey. 'From the catwalk, the ocean appears to be a calm element. It's only when you descend into the living areas that you start to appreciate the full strength of the ocean and the ferocity of the waves,' says Jolson.

Designed over one level, with the exception of the garage, the form of the house is clearly outlined with horizontal floor and roof plates both constructed in galvanised post-form channels. Thick vertical precast concrete panels create a strong juxtaposition in the design. 'The house was designed as a viewing platform,' says Jolson. And while the views are impressive, the architects were also mindful of the ever-changing weather patterns. A large outdoor deck was inserted on the more protected side of the site.

For the interior, bamboo was used extensively, from the floors to the joinery. 'Bamboo is incredibly strong, there's no movement in bamboo and it's particularly refined,' says Jolson, who also used bamboo to create a datum line across the living room wall. 'It mimics the horizon line of the ocean,' he adds.

Tower House

LAHZ NIMMO ARCHITECTS

Photography by Brett Boardman

This beach house at Casuarina Beach is only an hour's drive from Brisbane airport. Located in northern New South Wales, the position attracted the owner, an American working in Singapore. 'Our client was looking for a place he could occasionally use. He also wanted a house that he could rent out,' says architect Andrew Nimmo, a co-director of Lahz Nimmo Architects.

Casuarina Beach has undergone a significant transformation in the last few years. Once a sand mine, the land was purchased by developers who reinstated the sand dunes and subdivided the land for housing and commercial facilities. This house is located on the highest point of the area.

The 'tower' concept formed part of the client's brief. 'He saw it like having a tree-house,' says Nimmo, who initially tried to persuade his client to think again. 'Towers aren't often used, with access being one of the problems,' he adds. However, as a rental proposition, as well as a home, the tower has proved successful. 'People know it as the tower house. And they're keen to stay there. It's become a landmark building,' says Nimmo. Another request from the client was to include a self-contained bedroom. 'He wanted a room that he could stay in, even if it was for just a night'.

While the house appears relatively large from the street, it is actually quite compact. On the ground floor are two bedrooms and a bathroom, together with a double-height entry foyer. One of the bedrooms on the ground floor was designated as a 'bunk room', designed to accommodate several beds, or alternatively could be divided into two, further down the track.

Upstairs are the kitchen, dining and living areas, with a stairwell leading from the living area to the tower. The external staircase, enclosed with timber battons, appears almost to have been 'clipped on' to the house. The house is made of ivory concrete block work, rough-sawn plywood and fibro cement.

One of the most used parts of the house is the large deck separating the main bedroom from the kitchen and dining area. 'It's the coolest place in the house. You get all the sea breezes. It's also protected from the sun,' says Nimmo. 'It enjoys the finest views, with the dunes on one side and the swimming pool on the other'.

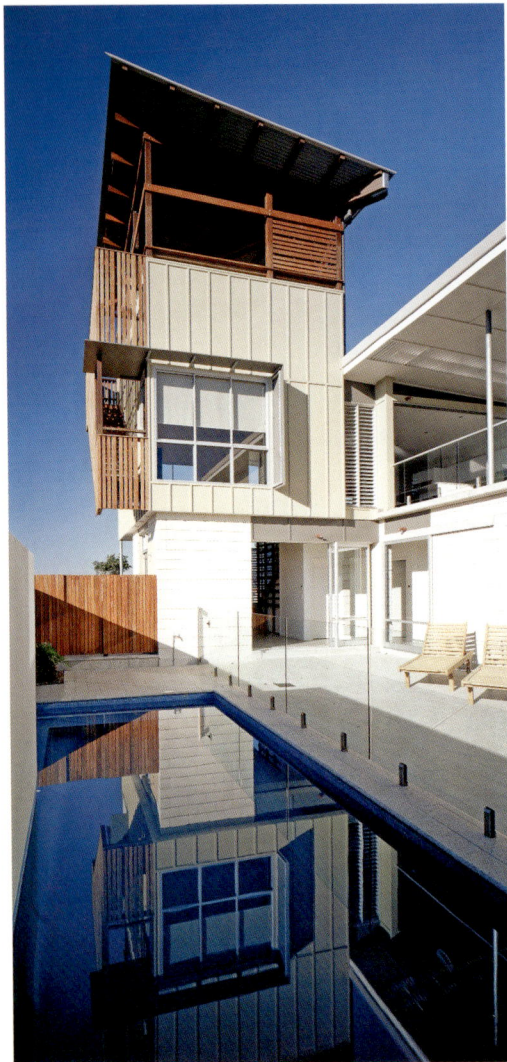

Framed by a National Park

LIPPMANN PARTNERSHIP

Photography by Willem Rethmeier

A national park on one side and a sheltered beach on the other border, Pearl Beach lies on the New South Wales central coast. Unlike many rural townships that have developed at an unprecedented pace, Pearl Beach has no plans for expansion. 'There are only a couple of hundred houses. The only change is the type of house now being built,' says architect Ed Lippmann.

The original 1950s beach shack was replaced with a 300-square-metre home made of glass, steel and fibre cement. Designed over two levels, the architect created a journey from the home's front entrance to the generous glazed rear facades. 'I wanted the view of the sea and the headlands to slowly unfold rather than be presented immediately past the front door,' says Lippmann, who skewed the main corridor leading to the kitchen, living and dining areas, located to the rear of the house.

Designed for a couple that regularly has family and friends to stay, the house includes two guest bedrooms on the ground floor, together with bathroom facilities. On the first floor is the main bedroom, walk-in dressing area, ensuite and separate office. 'Our clients regularly work from here. Eventually, their aim is to retire at Pearl Beach,' says Lippmann, who was conscious of creating a comfortable home as well as a beach side retreat.

While the large open-plan-kitchen and living areas provide panoramic views over the water towards Mount Ettalong, it's the courtyard space that provides the focal point of the owner's activities. 'I see this design as more of a courtyard house. Glass walls protect this courtyard that is adjacent to the living area. But it's completely open to the sky,' says Lippmann. 'It's protected from the winds,' he adds. And to blur the lines between the lounge and courtyard, hoop pine joinery appears in both spaces.

Lippmann was also conscious of the need to ventilate the spaces within the home. While the large sliding glass doors leading to the rear deck are regularly open, so is the glass pivot front door (located behind a fixed screen). 'Air is always moving through the houses, whether along the main corridor or through the highlight windows in the main living area,' says Lippman. And although the house is on a fairly modest site of approximately 650 square metres, there's a sense of endless vistas, with the sand and water stretching out in the distance.

Geometrical Wonder

MCBRIDE CHARLES RYAN

Photography by John Gollings

The owners of this beach house were after something completely different from their city home, a traditional Californian Bungalow. Located in Rye, on Victoria's Mornington Peninsula, the house designed by McBride Charles Ryan (MCR) Architects couldn't be more dissimilar.

Designed for a couple with three children, the house was partially inspired by the 'Klein Bottle', a model of a surface developed by German 19th-century mathematician Felix Klein. 'In principal, it's like a doughnut. You can twist and distort it, but it will only change topographically if it's cut. In a sense, there's no beginning or end,' says architect Rob McBride, who worked closely with his partner, interior designer Debbie-Lyn Ryan.

The house is made of compressed cement sheets with a black metal roof, which folds down in part to form an external wall. Moonah trees, with gnarled blackened trunks, anchor the house to the steeply sloping site. 'We wanted to evoke a sense of the fibro cement beach shacks in the area. We didn't want to make the house feel too precious,' says McBride. A front door, clad in cork, not only creates an unusual entrance, but also alludes to a cork stuck in a bottle.

When the 'cork' is removed, a bright red staircase and walls appear, like liquid solidified around an irregular-shaped lightwell. The entry lobby and laundry are at ground level. And although not apparent from the front façade, there's camouflaged back door providing access to a central courtyard.

There are no distinct separate levels; instead the rooms splay off the staircase around the central void. As you ascend the staircase there is a large flexible space that functions as a rumpus room and extra room for the children's friends to stay over. Continuing up there are two additional bedrooms and two bathrooms.

To maximise the light, as well as the views over the trees, the open-plan kitchen and living areas are located at the termination of the staircase, as is the main bedroom, a few steps above the living areas. Like the façade, the ceilings fold around the spaces like origami; likewise the fireplace, which appears 'folded' in one corner of the room.

The brief to MCR was for a joyous house, one that liberated the senses. And like a great party, where the bottle is left uncorked, the front door is regularly open to extended family and friends.

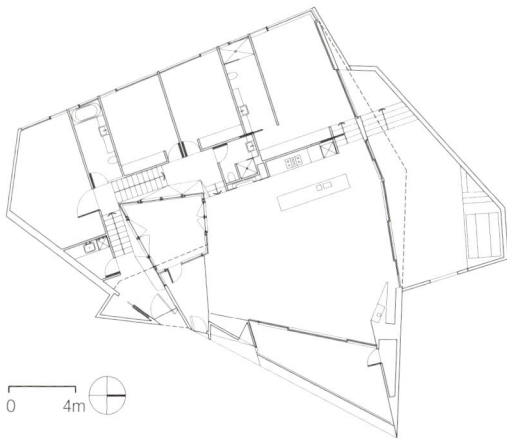

0   4m

Island Luxury

MELETITIKI-ALEXANDROS N. TOMBAZIS AND ASSOCIATES

Photography by Nikos Danielides

Spetses is a small, pine-covered island at the entrance of the Gulf of Argolis, 24 kilometres from the coast of the Peleponnese. The house lies on the southeast coastline, and is surrounded by 4,150 square metres of land, which slopes gently southwards to the sea.

The entrance to this property is from the northwest, via a cobblestone path that leads to the wooden gate of the inner courtyard, through which one enters the house. Passing through the semi-covered spaces of the courtyard and the arcade, the view to the southern courtyard, pool, and the sea is gradually revealed.

The house consists of three rectangular blocks. The two main ones, one with two floors and a tiled roof, and the other with one floor, are laid out at right angles defining the main, southeastern courtyard with the pool. The two buildings are connected at ground level by a semi-covered passage/arcade, on the roof of which a terrace with unimpeded views in all directions is created. The third block is a small pavilion used for dining al fresco.

Blue Sky and Ocean

ODDEN RODRIGUES ARCHITECTS

Photography by Robert Frith

This house is only an hour's drive south of Perth's CBD. 'The area will soon be an outer suburb,' says architect Simon Rodrigues. Overlooking Avalon Point and with views to the Indian Ocean, the house is slightly oriented to the northwest. 'You get the winter sun as well as unimpeded views directly ahead,' he adds.

While the house is on the fringe of town, it still enjoys unspoilt coastal heath and dune vegetation. 'It's relatively low-lying and often quite windy,' says Rodrigues. The brief to the architects was for a simple and sturdy house for a couple with three young children. 'One of the owners spent summer holidays in the area. They wanted something quite robust, like many of the homes built in the 1960s and 70s. They didn't want a townhouse on the coast,' he adds.

While it isn't made of fibro cement and perched on stilts like homes of that period, the house is relatively simple, both in form and materials used. Made from concrete tilt panels, galvanised steel beams, concrete floors and a steel roof, the house extends over three levels. Part of the ground floor is nestled into the sand dunes, with half this level almost submerged. This bunker-like area includes storage for rubber dinghies, fishing gear, a pool table and car parking. Craypots and an endless number of surfboards are also housed in this area.

The first level, oriented to the beach, contains five bedrooms, including the main bedroom that leads to a terrace. To maximise views, the living areas are on the top level. The open-plan kitchen, living and dining area includes dramatic picture windows. Divided by a viewing platform that's accessed by a ladder, the vista includes a rich palette of blues, from the ocean to the sky.

This beach house has a strong industrial aesthetic. Floors are concrete, as are many of the walls. And some of the doors are made of steel. 'The owners found many of the fittings in second-hand yards,' says Rodrigues, pointing out the stainless steel basins in the bathrooms. Some of the artifacts, such as the art in the living area, once appeared behind a hotel bar in Perth. 'The house is really quite restrained. I didn't want the house to compete with this view. It's essentially the blue sky and the ocean,' says Rodrigues modestly.

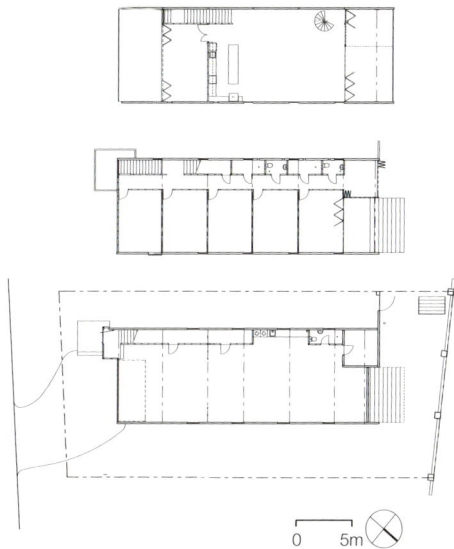

0 5m

Single-storey Treasure

OPTIMUM RESOURCE ARCHITECTS

Photography by Robert Frith, Acorn Photo Agency

This was one of those rare occasions when clients consult their architect about the purchase of a property. And it was also one of the best 'finds' in Western Australia's vast continuum of 'beachside' suburb developments.

The property has its long side boundary providing northern orientation over public open space, natural dunes and the sea to the west, and is at the end of a cul de sac.

A condition of purchase was the requirement that the building be single-storey – to preserve the views of the properties behind – with a minimum 20-degree pitched roof.

The 230-square-metre house was constructed using conventional and economical materials. A polished concrete floor throughout provides a surface that is both aesthetically interesting and easy to maintain, and is the only concession to luxury.

A series of reconstituted limestone block piers stretch along the northern façade. Sliding past the front of the limestone blocks are seven large aluminium-framed glass doors, which can be opened to take full advantage of the cool ocean winds, bringing the outside world in and opening the inside out towards the beach.

The extensive glazed wall to the west, protected by its 6-metre-deep verandah, allows the living area to be intimately connected with its surroundings and magnificent views of the evening sunset. Appropriate overhangs to the eaves keep out the unwanted summer sun, while the thermal mass and excellent wall-to-opening ratio result in an internal climate that is comfortable all year round.

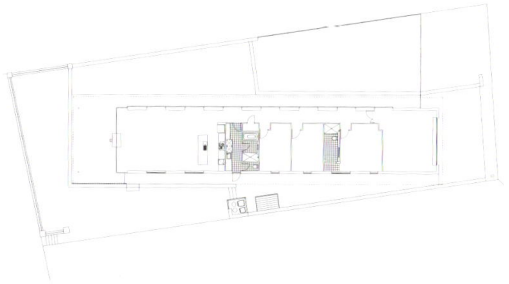

A Beachside Narrative

PARSONSON ARCHITECTS

Photography by Paul McCredie

This is a beach house for a family of five, located on the Kapiti Coast, north of Wellington. The intention was for the house to create a story of passage, from suburbia to the beach and the horizon beyond.

From the street, the house appears as a slightly ad hoc arrangement of separated forms, with hardiflex boxes anchored to the ground and lighter forms floating around the side, leading through to the beach. The living area is a raised pavilion from which to enjoy the hot summers and views of the sea.

Metaphors related to the location are threaded through the design, some are literal and some very abstract. These are present as one passes through or stays in the house, adding a resonance that is not necessarily fully discovered.

The house is close to the beach and exposed to the prevailing northwesterly winds. A pallete of non-corrosive materials have been used and are designed to weather.

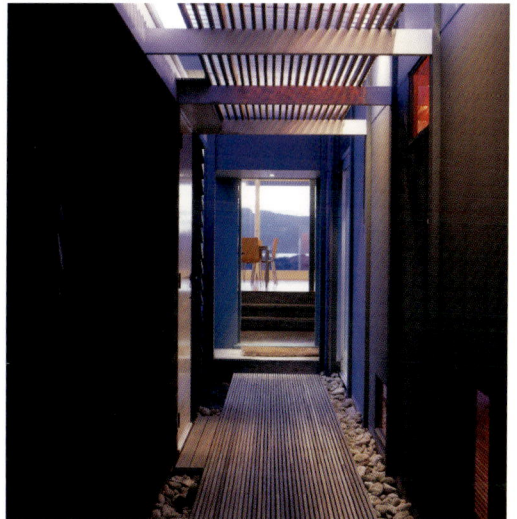

Washed Ashore

PARSONSON ARCHITECTS

Photography by Paul McCredie

The house is located at Pekapeka Beach, a small seaside settlement one hour's drive north of Wellington. It is a small one-bedroom house for a working couple who work in Wellington and Palmerston North.

The house is set on gently undulating dune lands, facing northwest, looking across the road and lower dunes out to the Tasman Sea and Kapiti Island to the west. It is intended that the house both relate to the horizontality of this landscape and also be at odds with it, as if it had been left there, or washed up.

The exterior is composed of a rhythm of painted fibre cement panels. Elements of wall, roof beam, roof layers and brise soleil are expressed separately, with light entering in places in between. There is a sense of horizontal and vertical layering, and metaphorically a sense of dislocation or decomposition of parts, as if a creature or construction had been left high and dry above the tide.

A Moveable Feast

PAUL UHLMANN ARCHITECTS

Photography by David Sandison Photography

This lightweight beach house was designed as a weekender for a city-based family. The site is 100 metres from the beach and faces west over a tea-tree-coloured creek. The local council regulations stipulate that the building must be able to be removed, by four-wheel-drive vehicle, within 12 hours of the sea reaching 50 metres from the property boundary. This requirement informed the house design, comprising small building pods that can be relocated.

To increase the exterior useable area, a series of fabric roof structures were designed to float above the lightweight buildings. Extensive timber decking provides links between the building pods as well as a large central outdoor living space. The fabric roofs provide a soft lighting level throughout the building, reminiscent of a campsite.

The building's walls were designed as a series of sandwich panels that fit within a standard window framing system, creating a gridded articulation to both the internal and external wall surface. Adjustable timber screening is used extensively to provide privacy, security and solar control. The landscape incorporates local plant species and white beach sand to capture the dunal qualities of the area.

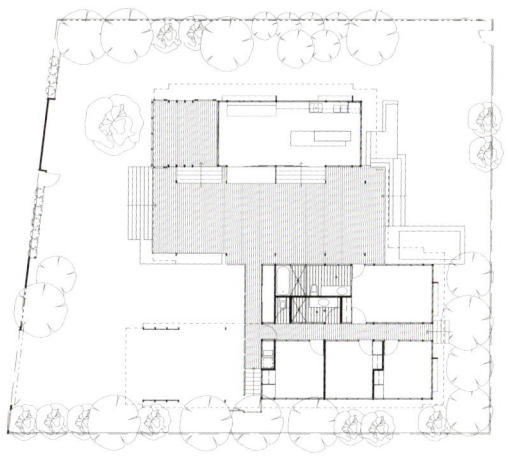

The Wave

PAUL UHLMANN ARCHITECTS

Photography by Aperture Architectural Photography

The site for this beach house is a narrow, steep block with spectacular views to the north and east over the Pacific Ocean. The house has been designed over three levels with a free-standing studio pod surrounded by trees at the bottom of the site.

The ground floor accommodates the living areas and kitchen with the terrace and pool along the northeast face. The master bedroom and ensuite are on the first floor, dramatically cantilevering over the pool. The basement accommodates four bedrooms, each with an ensuite bathroom, a large rumpus room and a laundry.

Circulation is along the east–west axis, providing differing views of the ocean and pool while traversing the three levels. Materials including stained timber cladding, white render and sandstone were chosen to weather and soften over time and to blend with the coastal landscape.

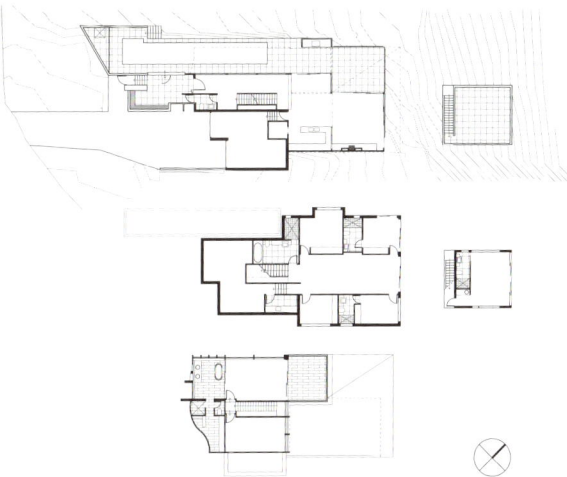

T - Shaped

PETE BOSSLEY ARCHITECTS

Photography by Patrick Reynolds

Crashing surf makes its presence felt in this beach house. And the noise of the surf competes with the strong winds. 'It's a fairly exposed site. There is not a great deal of vegetation for a windbreak,' says architect Pete Bossley, who, along with Andrew Bell, designed this T-shaped house for a couple with four children.

While there are several beach houses along the shoreline, this house, perched high on the embankment, appears to be on its own. The T-shape was considered an appropriate response to the severity of the wind, allowing a more protected aspect behind the exposed living areas that embrace the site.

The owners and guests arrive at a more sheltered part of the site and can park their cars undercover. A paved entrance leads past the children's bedroom wing and directly into the main pavilion that is divided between the kitchen, dining and living areas on one side and the main bedroom and guest bedroom and bathroom facilities on the other.

The living area leads to a large timber deck that features a 'catwalk', essentially a protruded walkway. 'We wanted to lead your eye out into the landscape. Even when the weather turns, it can be quite exhilarating to venture right out to the edge,' says Bossley, who says some of the most dramatic qualities of the home appear when a storm is about to break. 'We wanted to create the same excitement within the house,' says Bossley, who set up strong horizontal lines within the interior to create different perspectives of the hills and sea.

The beach house, which is made of steel and glass, features a lightweight skillion-shaped roof. And while the house appears relatively lightweight, especially in this environment, it is firmly anchored to the site by a rendered concrete plinth. As Bossley says, 'We saw the house as a viewing platform. It was designed to take a back seat to the landscape'.

Honeymoon Point

PHILP LIGHTON ARCHITECTS

Photography by Richard Eastwood

The location of this beach house would make most newlyweds swoon. Thirty kilometres from the nearest town, Honeymoon Point is sparsely populated and surrounded by natural bushland. This house is only one of four on this part of the secluded coastline. 'Originally the land was inaccessible. After it rained, the road was completely washed out,' says architect Tim Penny of Philp Lighton Architects.

Fortunately, locals redirected the road to higher ground, making this site a proposition. For the owners, a professional couple, it was an opportunity to enjoy a different experience from the city. 'Our clients wanted a beach house that was quite distinctive. They didn't want it to just disappear in the landscape,' says Penny.

The two-storey timber house is clad in rough-sawn timber. Internally, the house is simply finished hoop pine, with expressed timber beams. 'It's a simple design. The finishes are quite raw. It was designed so that a carpenter could build the entire house,' says Penny, who appreciated the remote location and the difficulty in attracting tradesmen to the property. While the timber house is fairly rudimentary (partially due to a limited budget), it is still sufficiently robust to endure the ferocious winds and constant rain. A corrugated-steel roof amplifies the sound of the rain.

The beach house includes a bedroom, bathroom and external storeroom on the ground level, flanked by two large timber decks. A stair leads to the first floor, which features a large living area, a galley-style kitchen, a study and main bedroom. There is a large deck leading from the study and living areas, offering panoramic views of the ocean. 'It isn't a precious house. Unlike honeymooners, the owners have two children. They can drag their gear up from the beach and clean the sand off on the decks,' says Penny, who likens the experience to camping. 'When the trees around the house become more established they'll feel even more part of the landscape'.

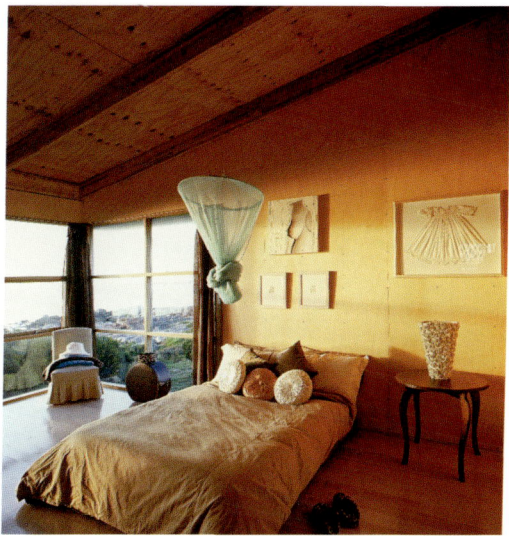

Seamless Transitions

SHUBIN + DONALDSON ARCHITECTS

Photography by Tom Bonner

This beachside modern house is perched along Malibu's Pacific Coast Highway and features access to the beach at the rear. A transitional interior entry courtyard introduces the primary design element of the home – a seamless union between interior and exterior spaces, with crisp linear architecture and visual access throughout.

From the entry courtyard, an original space accented by a grid of windowpanes houses the dining room. The grid is echoed by the geometric pattern of the cabinets and shelves that lead into the minimal kitchen. True to the open plan, the kitchen overlooks the main living space.

The ground-floor living room and adjacent sitting room offer respite from the sunlit terraces beyond, with cooling white and dark wood tones in the furniture and materials. Double-paned windows, which open onto the first-level terrace, permit unrestricted views onto the ocean while buffering sound from the highway.

The upstairs rooms continue the overall theme of air, light and water with repeating materials and colours. The master suite faces onto a second large terrace with pocket-glass doors that fold away, converting the stepped upper terrace into a sleeping porch. Openness and transformation are themes throughout and are most expressive in the master bath, where cool, ocean-blue frosted glass lines the walls and windows. Three layers of floor-to-ceiling glass form a translucent door that closes the space off from the bedroom, or opens it up to the master suite, porch, and Pacific Ocean beyond. Dark wenge wood – used throughout the house as an accent – encases the tub, vanity and spacious closets. Double mirrors are placed on poles in front of the frosted glass, rather than set into a wall.

A Great Opportunity

SJB ARCHITECTS

Photography by Tony Miller

This property at St Andrews Beach, Victoria, was vacant for a considerable time. While the tea-treed site, set in the dunes, was only a short distance from the surf beach, it was unusually steep, falling approximately 13 metres from the road. Height control limits set by the local council also deterred prospective purchasers. However, for the owners, a couple with young children, the property excited them from first inspection. 'I tried to share their excitement. But I was cautious about the challenges ahead,' says architect Alfred de Bruyne, a director of SJB Architects.

While de Bruyne was looking at ways to build a beach house, the owners were talking romantically about the classic Aussie beach house: restrained, honest, simple and easy to live in. 'They wanted the children to be able to return to the house with sand between their toes, not worrying about bringing it into the house,' says de Bruyne.

From the street, the house appears as a single storey. Clad in copper, it is closed to the street. 'Copper was an ideal material. It stands up to the salt air. It always has a wonderful patina,' says de Bruyne, who included large timber sleepers in the forecourt to create a similar rustic feel.

Past the glass-and-timber door, the house opens up to the view. The top level, also the point of access, includes a separate family room at the front of the house. This room, used by the children, is separated from the open-plan kitchen, dining and living area by an internal courtyard. 'We wanted to get northern light into the house. But we also wanted to create separation between the two living areas,' says de Bruyne. A large terrace, accessed via stackable glass doors, extends the indoor space. A staircase adjacent to the kitchen leads to the lower level: a main bedroom, ensuite, a study, three bedrooms and a bathroom, accessed both externally and internally.

While the house appears moody from the street, the interior is light and transparent. Highlight clerestory windows hover above the kitchen, and the living area is framed by glass on three sides. And although the house appears relatively modest in scale from the street, it is in reality a large family weekender. 'The children love it. There's a play area in the backyard. But as the land falls away, there are also pockets below the house for the children to explore'.

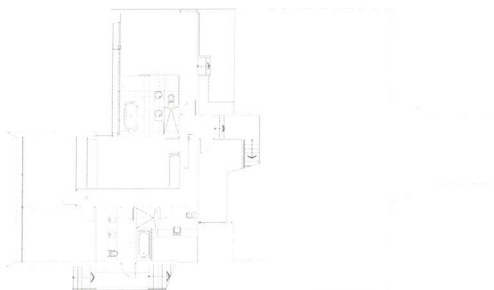

Lower ground floor plan

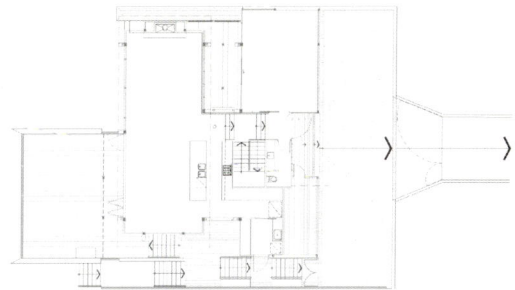

Ground floor plan

A Panoramic View

SJB ARCHITECTS AND SJB INTERIORS

Photography by Tony Miller

Few beach houses enjoy such a privileged position. A mere 25 metres from the water, this house overlooks grassy sand dunes and is one of only a handful along the water's edge. Replacing an old beach shack with a new house gave SJB Architects and SJB Interiors an opportunity to match the design to the location. The focus is on the beach, the bay and the sand dunes.

The owners, who have grown-up children, not only wanted a design commensurate with the view, but also a house that could be used when the children weren't there. 'They didn't want to be greeted with a series of large rooms that weren't going to be occupied,' says architect Alfred de Bruyne. So the architects created two living zones that could be occupied independently of each other.

On the top floor are the main bedroom, ensuite, kitchen and living area. On the ground floor are three bedrooms, main kitchen and living area. Both levels have generous access to the outdoor areas. On the ground level, the walls of the house are extended to frame the outdoor areas, creating privacy and protection from the wind. And on the second level, there is a continuous outdoor deck that wraps around the entire space. While the outdoor space, framed with glass balconies, appears exposed to the elements, a retractable awning on the roof can be used for protection. 'It's automated. You can quickly batten down when the weather changes,' says de Bruyne.

The façade is clad in western red cedar. Crisp and contemporary, it presents a modest face to the street. However, once through the front door, full-length glass windows face the view. As de Bruyne says, 'The design celebrates the position. It's a regular-sized block, but you don't feel as if you are hemmed in. The neighbour's front gardens are part of the larger picture. You could be simply anywhere.'

On a Ridge

SORENSEN ARCHITECTS

Photography by Olivier Marill

This house is located in the Cape Region of Western Australia. Approximately 270 kilometres south of Perth, the house looks towards the Indian Ocean on one side and Geographe Bay on the other. 'It was previously used for farming. The area was overgrazed and some of the topsoil has blown away over the years,' says architect Michael Sorensen.

The 7-hectare property has few neighbours. With strict council guidelines, including a height restriction (5 metres), those seeking large double-storey homes stay away. 'The landscape is slowly regenerating. I was mindful of the grass trees and unique landscape when designing this house,' says Sorensen, who was not deterred by the height limit.

Built for a family, the house was designed to be used every weekend or two. 'The owners wanted to be able to open the door, quickly unpack and relax. They didn't want to have a list of tasks to attend to,' says Sorensen, who has extensive local knowledge and a practice at Margaret River, 30 kilometres south of the site.

The single-storey rendered brick house is painted a green-grey colour, in keeping with hues in the landscape. As the northwest and southwest winds are strong, the house includes curved roofs as well as protected courtyards. 'The roofs deflect the wind,' says Sorensen, who also incorporated two courtyards, a large half-walled summer courtyard and a high brick-walled winter retreat in the design.

While the house appears relatively modest in the landscape, it is reasonably spacious, measuring approximately 350 square metres. Following a staggered H-plan, the kitchen, dining and living areas occupy the northern tip of the H, as does the children's rumpus room. A service pod, including the bathrooms and garage, forms the cross of the H, with the main and children's bedrooms located on the southern portion.

Although there are some coastal views from the living areas, the premier aspect is found on three rooftop decks. The central deck is covered by a roof. 'It's a great place for alfresco dining or simply just looking out to the ocean,' says Sorensen.

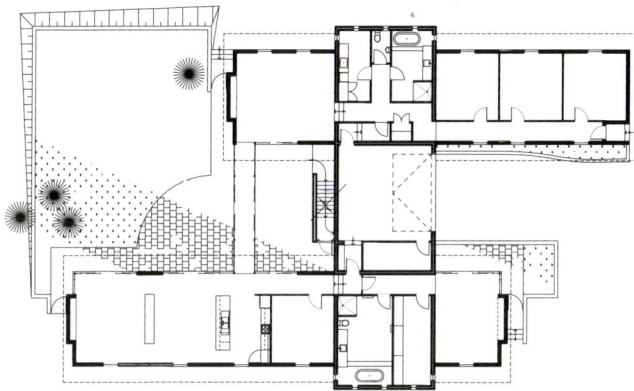

A Great Beach House

STUDIO 101 ARCHITECTS

Photography by Trevor Mein

There were few meetings required to determine the design of this beach house, in Lorne, Victoria. The clients, a couple based in Noosa, responded to the architect's emails, as well as the occasional phone-call. 'The brief was essentially to "design a great beach house",' says architect Peter Woolard, director of Studio 101 Architects.

Rather than create a solid mass on the steep site, which falls approximately 10 metres towards the street, Studio 101 Architects designed a lightweight structure. Conceived as two pavilions supported by steel beams, the cypress-clad beach house appears to float above the property. 'We didn't want the house to interfere with the vegetation or the natural watercourses on site,' says Woolard, pointing out the space under the house to allow water to pass. 'The house was also elevated to allow for natural ventilation, benefiting from the sea breezes,' he adds.

Woolard designed the two pavilions with the living pavilion 'slipping' past the sleeping pavilion. The entry point acts as a breezeway. Framed with a timber and glass door on one side and a floor-to-ceiling glass louvred window on the other, the irregular shaped lobby is an interstitial space. 'When the door and louvres are open, you feel as though you're sitting on a verandah,' says Woolard, who also used the entrance to separate the living areas from the three bedrooms.

The main kitchen and living areas are defined by a change in level, one of five in the house. The changes in level are only slight, but they allow for a journey through the house rather than one direct path to the water ahead. 'In a sense the two pavilions have been cranked on the site to enliven the experiences,' says Woolard.

A small viewing platform leads from the lounge. From the kitchen, a more internalised deck is protected from behind by the second pavilion. 'We've still maintained the view of the sea. But we were also conscious of providing an outdoor space that could be used. The winds down here can be fairly strong and unpredictable,' says Woolard.

While the house can be likened to a suitcase (opened up on arrival), the design is considerably more complicated. It may appear as a simple beach house but in reality the house has been finely crafted to the site and oriented to fully benefit from the path of the sun as well as the sea views.

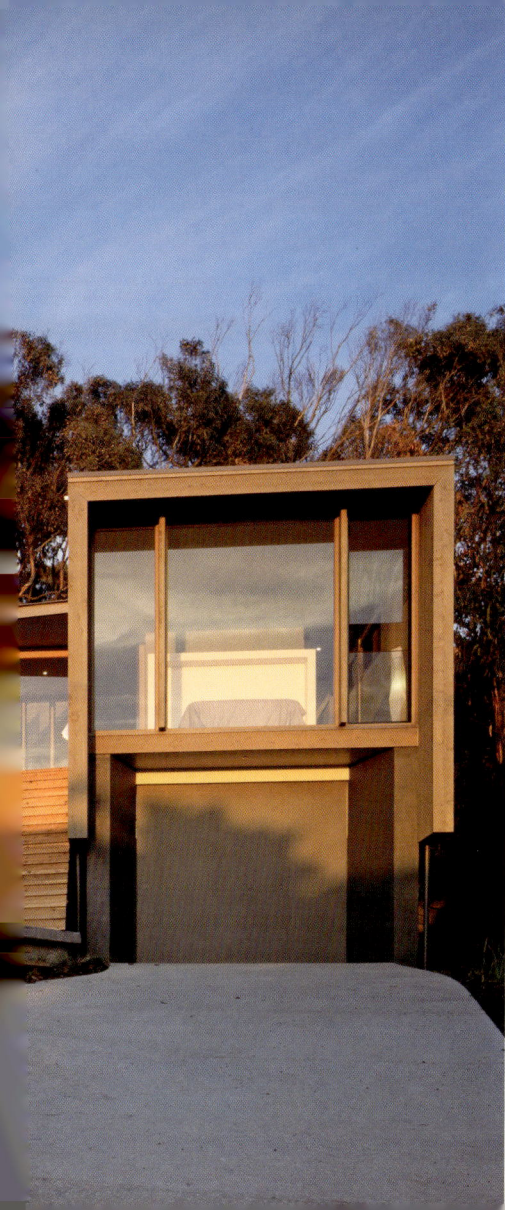

A New Life

STUDIO 101 ARCHITECTS

Photography by Trevor Mein

It's difficult to reconcile this beach house at Lorne, Victoria, with its previous incarnation, a simple, single-storey beach shack that offered glimpses of Loutitt Bay. 'The house had been owned by the family for several years. A few minor alterations had been made, such as the upgrade of the kitchen,' says architect Peter Woolard, director of Studio 101 Architects.

Owned by a couple with two adult children, the brief to the architects was to maximise views to the north, aligned to the bay. They also wanted to integrate the indoor and outdoor spaces, particularly as the land slopes 5 metres down from the road at the front of the property. 'Our clients also asked for a separate living area for their children, a place where they could entertain friends,' says Woolard.

Initial client discussions centred on retaining the original house and extending it. 'We thought about knocking it over completely. But the existing footprint set up the planning parameters. If we started from scratch, we might have been required to build further down the site, thereby reducing the water views,' says Woolard. The original freestanding garage, located to one side of the house, was converted into a living area for the two children. Floor-to-ceiling glass doors were inserted in the garage's north wall, leading to a new timber deck. A kitchenette and a bathroom were also included in the new quarters.

Substantial changes were made to the original house. The ground and only floor of the original home was completely reworked. It now comprises four bedrooms, including the main bedroom with ensuite, a bathroom and a separate powder room. The bathrooms are clearly delineated with recycled timber battens, which also form a feature wall for a new staircase.

The new first floor is also clearly delineated. Constructed in timber, the first floor is adorned with Rheinzink panels. 'The Rheinzink captures the colour of the landscape. The ribs in the zinc cast their own shadows on the house,' says Woolard, who was also keen to reduce the scale of the first-floor addition. Upstairs, there is a large open-plan kitchen, living and dining area, flanked to the north by floor-to-ceiling glass doors and windows. And to attract additional light, highlight windows wrap around the living areas. And rather than glimpses of water through tree trunks, there are panoramic views from numerous vantage points, both inside and on the terraces outside the home.

In Context

SWANEY DRAPER ARCHITECTS

Photography by Trevor Mein

This property at Barwon Heads, Victoria, had been in the same family for years. Only half an hour away from Geelong, it's surrounded by rolling sand dunes and a golf course. With Bass Strait providing the backdrop, the property feels considerably more isolated than it actually is. Perched on a hill, the beach house enjoys panoramic views to the hinterlands, Bass Strait and the Barwon River.

The design brief included respecting the 1920s clubhouse on the adjacent golf course. 'They didn't want to recreate the 1920s building. It was a case of acknowledging its existence,' says architect Simon Swaney, who worked closely with architect Sally Draper. 'There's quite a lot of family history associated with the property. The owner didn't want a beach house that looked as though it had just been erected in days,' adds Swaney.

Drawing upon the local moonah trees as well as the clubhouse, the architects used materials that suggested context. Rammed earth walls, drawn from a local quarry, form the basis for one of the pavilions in the home. The other pavilions feature grey weathered timbers, and all the pavilions feature pitched roofs, like the 1920s clubhouse.

The house comprises one long two-storey pavilion and a smaller pavilion. The large pavilion contains the main bedroom on the first floor, and the kitchen, service area and an area for bunk beds on the ground floor. 'It's quite a solid pavilion. It's south-facing and receives the harshest winds,' says Swaney. In contrast, the other pavilions face north and are considerably lighter in feel. These single-storey pavilions contain the living areas, one formal, the other informal. Bridging the two living spaces is the dining area, leading to a large timber deck.

In contrast to the living spaces, with pitched roofs and limed timber trusses, the dining area features a flat ceiling. 'The dining area is pivotal to the design. It brings the family together. It also connects the views of the water to the golf green,' says Swaney, who framed views in some of the more exposed spaces. The long slot-style window in the formal living area allows privacy, while still maintaining views to the head of the river. 'It's quite an exposed site. But from inside, the views belong entirely to the owners,' he adds.

Designed to Last

SWANEY DRAPER ARCHITECTS

Photography by Trevor Mein

The sound of surf fills this house at Lorne, overlooking Victoria's Great Ocean Road. The crashing waves literally appear to be at the doorstep. 'Our clients had been looking for a site to build on for some time. They wanted to be slightly outside the township, and a little more isolated,' says architect Simon Swaney, who designed this house with architect Sally Draper.

The architects excavated 4 metres on the relatively steep site to nestle the house between neighbours. And to ensure privacy from the winding coastal road, a 3-metre cantilevered deck was added. 'Our clients didn't want to feel like goldfish in a bowl. This house is a retreat, not a city home,' says Swaney.

The brief was to create a large home that took advantage of the vista over Loutitt Bay. While the outlook from the lighthouse at Airey's Inlet to the pier at Lorne is impressive, so is the wind chill, particularly during the winter months. 'We knew we had to create a more temperate environment,' says Swaney, who created a protected rear courtyard as well as front decks. However, the architects were also mindful of not sacrificing water views for comfort. As a result, there are unimpeded views from the rear terrace and lawn through glass doors on either side of the living areas.

The house, clad in black-stained timber, features a striking 8-metre-high sandstone spine wall. Slicing the house into two, this wall also delineates bedrooms from living areas. The kitchen is placed to one side of the living area. The central island bench, made of stone, includes two sinks and occupies a premier position. The dining area features a cantilevered built-in window box. Externally framed by an aluminium 'picture frame', the seat with its large picture window is one of the most favoured spots in the house. Louvred blinds, operated automatically, ensure the amount of sunlight is controlled.

Spaces are carefully arranged over six levels. The children's play area, leading from the kitchen, is oriented to the north and rear courtyard. Featuring glass bi-fold doors, this room opens to a small patch of lawn. In contrast, the main bedroom occupies the top level of the house. Designed like a retreat, it features a built-in study at one end and an open-plan bathroom at the other.

This beach house has a timeless quality. 'It's not just about natural ventilation and using recycled materials. It's as important to design a building that lasts,' says Swaney.

The Great Outdoors

TIM DORRINGTON ARCHITECTS

Photography by Emma-Jane Hetherington

Located in a beachside subdivision in the far north, the 600-square-metre site is almost flat, with the beach a stone's-throw away. The 'suburban' nature of this site dictated the provision of as much privacy as possible, without compromising the available views and sunlight. The plan opens up to the north and west, capturing and maximising the best of both of these. The house consists of four main elements – a bedroom block, a living pavilion, a garage and the linking corridor.

The bedroom block contains a bunkroom, a rumpus room/fourth bedroom and the bathroom in the basement. The bathroom's concrete floor and block walls reference camping ablution blocks. Two main bedrooms, both with ensuite bathrooms, occupy the middle floor and on the top floor is a games room that doubles as a second living room.

The living pavilion sits apart to the north of the bedroom block and references a campsite in homage to the campground that occupied this area for many years. Two sides of the pavilion completely open up to provide the sense of casual living associated with the traditional Kiwi family camping holiday.

The garage is a bunker half-buried in the site, contrasting with the light and airiness of the living space. Sunk into the ground the same distance the living pavilion is raised up, the garage and basement of the bedroom block are linked to the rest of the house by the polycarbonate-clad corridor. This was conceived as a breezeway and works more as an exterior space, connecting the various elements of the house.

Landscaping has been kept to a minimum and is integrated into the house plan with gabion walls providing separation from neighbouring sites and acting as retaining walls for the raised and sunken gardens and the lawn ramp that rolls from the western side of the living pavilion.

The material palette reflects the tight budget of the project and also helps convey the camping reference. Bondor panels are used for the sloped roofs and in turn provide the ceilings. Clear-sealed concrete block and eterpan, corrugated polycarbonate sheet and plywood cladding, meranti and hoop pine ply cabinetry, and polished concrete floors provide a rustic natural palette. In practical terms these materials are all hard wearing and ensure easy care, perfect for a family beach house.

Off the Main Track

VLADIMIR IVANOV, ARCHITECT

Photography by Giles Westley

This quiet beach hamlet, three-and-a-half hour's drive from the city, is not widely known, except by locals. While the beaches are pristine, the housing stock hasn't moved on from the 1950s and 1960s. The choice is either the fibro shack or the modest red brick home, built a few years later. So when architect Vladimir Ivanov unveiled plans for a contemporary beach house, the locals thought they were getting a new restaurant. 'It's not a particularly large house. But compared to the neighbours, it appears quite monumental,' says Ivanov, who regularly fielded enquires as to the function of the building.

Approximately 300 square metres in area, the house sits prominently on its corner site, with two street frontages. Designed for a couple, who operate a dairy farm during the week, the brief included separate accommodation for a parent moving from interstate. 'Essentially my clients wanted two houses in one. But they wanted the design to appear as though it was one house from the street,' says Ivanov.

The house is conceived as three forms that interconnect. The first form, the self contained apartment, is legible from the street and consists of a box with a double masonry wall, clad with timber laminate. This form is interconnected to the main house, which comprises generous glazing at ground level and rendered masonry walls above. 'The timber box anchors the house, which is quite transparent,' says Ivanov.

The two-storey house features glazed windows on three sides and rendered masonry on the fourth, to prevent the harsher sunlight from entering the home. The open-plan kitchen and living areas on the ground floor have unimpeded views of the beach and pine trees. To ensure some privacy, Ivanov designed a series of seats/storage units made of fibro cement on the large deck, some featuring open shelves, others closed nooks. 'The owners love collecting shells and driftwood from the beach. They can either hide it away or display these on the open shelves,' says Ivanov.

Upstairs affords the same generous views of the water, particularly from the main bedroom and balcony. Ivanov also included a second bedroom, together with a study/third bedroom, should additional guests stay over. 'It's quite a simple design,' says Ivanov, who selected robust materials to allow for sand being bought into the house. As Ivanov says, 'I've provided extra-wide grooves for the timber deck. The sand can just be swept away'.

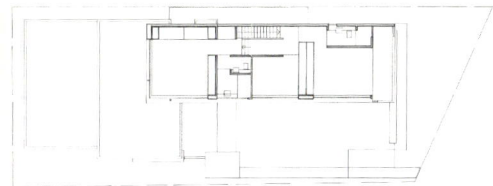

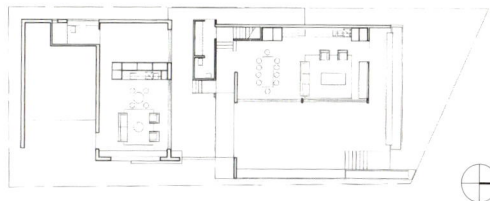

For Keen Surfers

WALTER BARDA DESIGN

Photography by Bart Maiorana

This house was made for keen surfers. Directly opposite a surf beach and exposed to the ocean, this house sits at the base of a lush tropical forest. 'The whole family surf. It's the reason why the house exists,' says architect Water Barda.

Constructed of stone and stained timber, the house features a corrugated steel roof, not dissimilar to many of the original beach houses remaining in the area. The two-storey house was built for a family and visiting guests and is loosely divided into two zones. On the ground floor are two large 'bunk' rooms for the children and their friends. On the opposite side, separated by a large outdoor timber deck is a billiard room.

On the first level are the kitchen, living and dining areas, together with the main bedroom and ensuite. Barda also included a *lanai* on the first floor, to allow guests the opportunity for an afternoon nap. 'The timber blinds can be pulled down if they choose to have a rest. But they can also use the space as a retreat during the day for reading,' says Barda, whose brief from the clients included creating a parent's or guest retreat. 'The afternoon nap is part of the ritual of taking holidays by the beach. The sound of the waves crashing is quite soothing,' he adds.

While the living areas on the first floor are open to each other, they have a sense of containment provided by vaulted ceilings in each space. 'We treated the spaces as a series of pavilions. Each ceiling has been expressed differently,' says Barda, pointing to the unique angles.

Also important in the design was to include protected outdoor areas, particularly as the ocean winds can be bitterly cold. Barda designed a large timber deck between the main bedroom and the living area, protected by a deep timber eave. There is also a deck at ground level that spills out onto the lawn. For the family that own this house, it's the prevailing surf that counts. As Barda says, 'The weather doesn't usually dictate when surf boards are taken out. This beach house is used all year around'.

A Touch of the South Pacific

WALTER BARDA DESIGN

Photography by Robert Morehead

This house in Whale Beach, on Sydney's northern beaches, has a slightly worn feel to it. Unlike the crisp white homes dotted along the coastline, this house merges into the landscape. 'It has quite a rustic feel. The colours and materials are recessive,' says architect Walter Barda.

Designed for a couple with three children, the brief was for a house with a touch of the South Pacific. 'The owners had been living in Brazil for several years and they travel extensively. They wanted the sense of an island home,' says Barda.

As the house is on a steep site, the land was prepared for a multi-level house – six levels in total. Considerable excavation was required to maximise the site, as well as the view. 'There are water views from most rooms,' says Barda, who was also keen to create a large outdoor terrace from the living areas.

To accommodate the slope, the house runs vertically rather than horizontally. Stairs lead from ground level to a guest bedroom, bathroom, home office and gymnasium. While there are glimpses of the water from this level, the heroic vista is from the kitchen and living areas on the level above, which also features a large outdoor terrace and corner lanai.

To accentuate the view, Barda created a double-height space over the living areas. Complete with exposed timber trusses and a massive stone fireplace, there's a sense of rustic grandeur. During the warmer weather, the large timber and glass sliding doors can be pulled back and highlight louvred glass windows opened.

Three levels were designed above the living areas. On the first level are the three children's bedrooms, together with a shared bathroom. A half level up is a mezzanine level, overlooking the living areas, used for watching television or simply reading. The main bedroom, ensuite and study are on the highest level. There is also a terrace with a swimming pool leading from this bedroom.

The materials chosen for the house are subtle and quite dark. Apart from the sandstone plinth, there is extensive use of timber, both new and recycled. Recycled timber posts feature prominently on a terrace and are overscaled in height and diameter. Shadow-clad timber also features, along with weatherboards. 'The house isn't supposed to look as though it was recently built,' says Barda.

A Sustainable Vision

WORKSHOP 1 DUNN + HILLAM ARCHITECTS

Photography by Kilian O'Sullivan

The brief for this project was to convert three apartments in two existing buildings into one family house that included a private area for the adults and a space to allow them to work from home. Two fundamental spatial requirements were to activate a private outdoor courtyard room and to protect the inhabitants from the view of people using the beach. A decision was made early in the project to retain the existing 1950s brick block building mass and work within its spatial framework. This allowed the architects to adapt the house to a sustainable future by engaging the thermal mass and utilising cross-ventilation and heat stack effects to control heat. Underground water storage and natural filtration systems were installed to use collected roof water for laundry, bathroom, garden and drinking needs.

The architecture has been expressed as a series of finely crafted, space-making furniture pieces that have been inserted into and grafted onto the fabric of the existing building. The window boxes in the living room and bedrooms puncture the envelope of the brick skin and create a new seat or table while providing protection from the sun and wind. The windows slide over the external elevation so that they disappear when viewed from the inside, and the new sunroom and northwestern wall have been wrapped around the brick mass. The northwestern wall uses a stack effect to passively cool the rest of the house. In the colder months the warm air is stored in the stairwell and then distributed around the house by fans.

All of the new joinery pieces have been made from recycled Australian hardwood (spotted gum) that had been retrieved from old wool stores and industrial buildings. The patina and grain of this beautiful timber gives a special quality to the spaces that were made in and around the house.

Connecting to the Sea

WRIGHT FELDHUSEN ARCHITECTS

Photography by Olivia Reeves

This house appears to merge with the sea. 'Our client is a keen swimmer. He wanted to be connected to the water, whether he was doing laps or relaxing inside,' says architect Tim Wright.

While the house enjoys 180-degree views of the water, there are houses directly in front. But as the house is perched on a hill, with a 6-metre fall of land from front to back, the vista isn't compromised by neighbouring homes. Relatively modest in size, the 500-square-metre site was subdivided by the owners. 'Split down the centre, two new houses enjoy unimpeded views,' says Wright.

Designed for a couple with two young children, the house is spread across three levels. Car parking and servicing equipment for the pool are at basement level. The kitchen, living and dining areas, a children's rumpus room, plus a guest bedroom and ensuite are on the first floor. On the second and top level are the main bedroom, dressing area and ensuite, as well as the children's bedrooms and laundry. As the site slopes towards the street, the laundry is aligned to ground level. Whether you're in the main bedroom or in the living areas, water can be enjoyed from most vantage points. 'Our clients wanted the house to be as transparent as possible,' says Wright.

To achieve this transparency, the house features extensive use of glass. Zinc cladding and off-form concrete also make up the range of materials used. Zinc, being a non-ferrous material, is rust resistant and an ideal material for projects close to the sea. 'The off-form concrete was poured to appear as though it had grown out of the site,' says Wright, pointing out the horizontal bands of concrete that form the base of the house, as well as in the walls of the double-height void enclosing the staircase. 'Our clients wanted a house that was low maintenance. But the house is fairly exposed, so concrete anchors the house to the site,' says Wright.

One of the most pleasurable activities for the owners of the house is using the pool, either for laps, or just for splashing in. 'You feel as though you're swimming out to sea,' says Wright, who cantilevered the main bedroom approximately 2 metres to strengthen the connection between house and water. 'It's only a rocky outcrop below. So the pleasure of the beach comes from gazing out through these windows,' he adds.

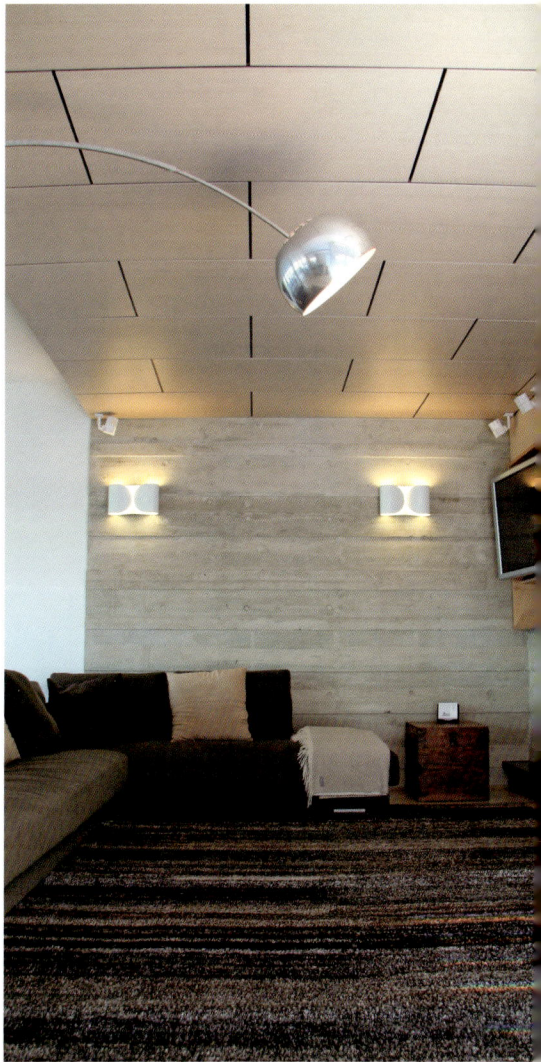

Architect Contact Details

Alex Popov & Associates
www.alexpopov.com.au

Anderson Architecture
www.andersonarchitecture.com.au

Ashton Raggatt McDougall
www.a-r-m.com.au

B.E. Architecture
www.bearchitecture.com

Bailey Architects
www.baileyarchitects.co.nz

Barclay & Crousse Architecture
www.barclaycrousse.com

Bellemo & Cat
www.bellemocat.com

Bevin + Slessor Architects
www.bevinslessor.co.nz

Bligh Voller Nield Architecture
www.bvn.com.au

BOORA Architects
www.boora.com

Centrum Architects
www.centrum.com.au

Cox Rayner Architects
www.cox.com.au

CPRW FISHER limited
www.cprwfisher.co.nz

Craig Steere Architects
www.craigsteerearchitects.com.au

Dale Jones-Evans Architects
www.dje.com.au

Daniel Marshall Architect
www.marshall-architect.co.nz

Daniela Simon Architect @ SODAA
www.sodaa.com.au

Donovan Hill Architects
www.donovanhill.com.au

George El Khouri Architects
www.elkhouri.com.au

Godward Guthrie Architecture
www.gga.co.nz

Greg Natale Design
www.gregnatale.com

Gregory Burgess Architects
www.gbarch.com.au

Hayball
www.hayball.com.au

Hayne Wadley Architects
www.haynewadley.com.au

Hulena Architects
www.hulena.com

Jolson
www.jolson.com.au

Lahz Nimmo Architects
www.lahznimmo.com

Lippmann Partnership
www.lippmann.com.au

McBride Charles Ryan
www.mcbridecharlesryan.com.au

Meletitiki-Alexandros N. Tombazis
and Associates
www.meletitiki.gr

Odden Rodrigues Architects
(see Rodrigues Bodycoat Architects and
Optimum Resource Architects)

Optimum Resource Architects
ora@iinet.net.au

Parsonson Architects
www.p-a.co.nz

Paul Uhlmann Architects
www.pua.com.au

Pete Bossley Architects
www.bossleyarchitects.co.nz

Philp Lighton Architects
www.philplighton.com.au

Rodrigues Bodycoat Architects
www.rba.architecture.net.au

Shubin + Donaldson Architects
www.shubinanddonaldson.com

SJB Architects
www.sjb.com.au

Sorensen Architects
www.sorensenarchitects.com.au

Studio 101 Architects
www.studio101.com.au

Swaney Draper Architects
sswaney@batessmart.com
sdraper@sallydraperarchitects.com.au

Tim Dorrington Architects
www.tdarchitects.co.nz

Vladimir Ivanov, Architect
www.vniarchitects.com.au

Walter Barda Design
www.walterbardadesign.com

Workshop 1 Dunn + Hillam Architects
www.workshop1.com.au

Wright Feldhusen Architects
www.wrightfeldhusen.com

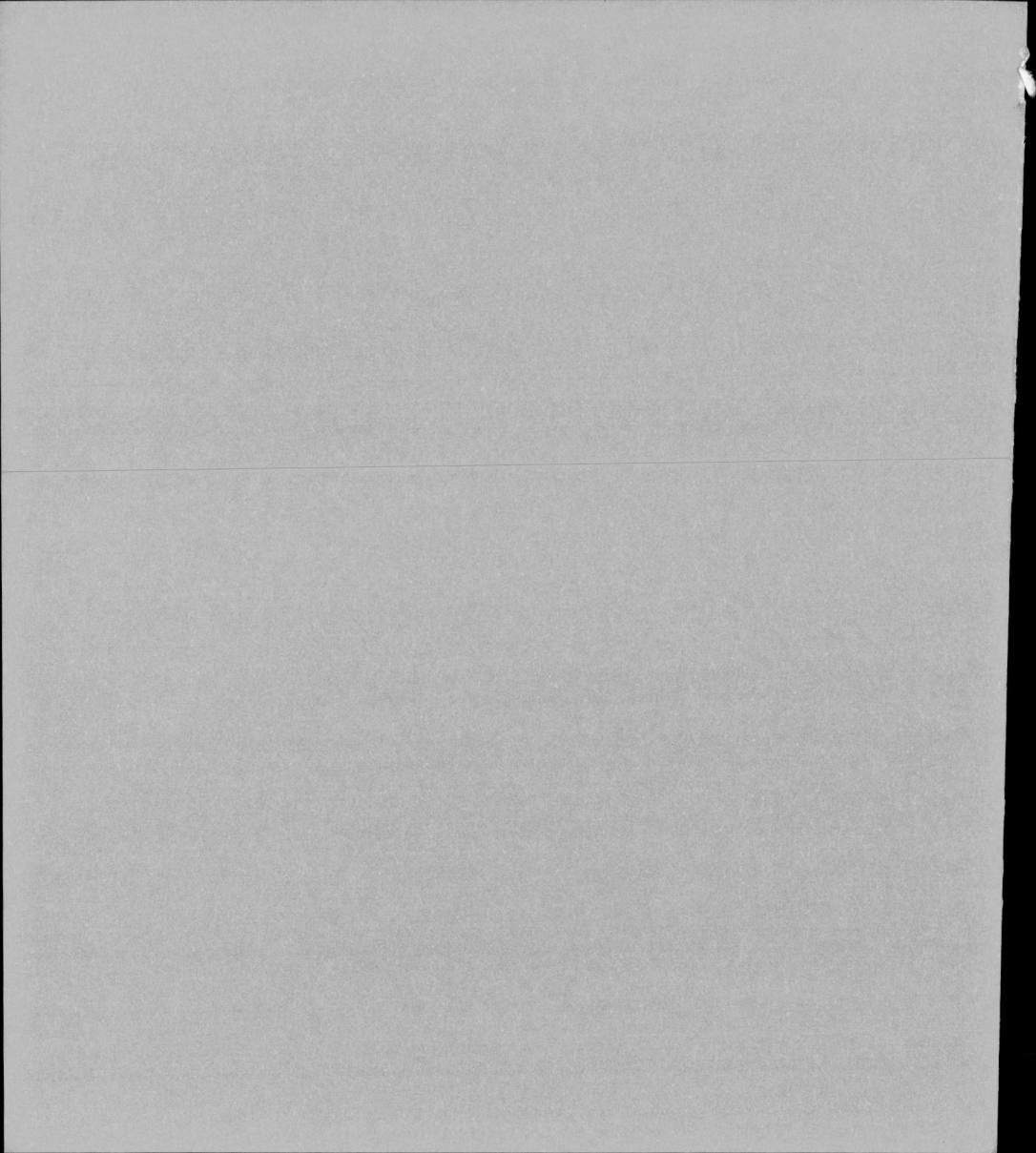